Asset-Based Mortgage Refinancing & Equity Access

How to Use Asset-Based Mortgage Loans for Cash-Out Refinancing and Liquidity

By Joseph G. Correa

Licensed Mortgage Broker, Finibi Mortgage

Copyright & Legal Notice

Published by Live Stronger Faster

The information provided in this book is for educational and informational purposes only and does not constitute financial, legal, tax, or investment advice. The author and publisher make no representations or warranties regarding the accuracy, completeness, or applicability of the content. Readers are encouraged to consult with licensed professionals, including mortgage lenders, financial advisors, tax professionals, and attorneys, before making any financial decisions.

The strategies and examples discussed in this book are illustrative in nature and may not be suitable for all individuals or situations. Results may vary based on market conditions, lender guidelines, and individual financial circumstances. The author and publisher are not responsible for any financial losses, decisions, or outcomes resulting from the use or misuse of the information contained in this book.

All trademarks, service marks, and product names referenced in this publication are the property of their respective owners and are used for identification purposes only.

First Edition, 2026

Table of Contents

Foreword

The traditional mortgage system was built on one central idea: income determines opportunity. For decades, borrowers were measured, filtered, and ultimately approved or denied based on how predictable and documentable their income appeared on paper. Yet in today's evolving financial landscape, this model no longer reflects the full picture of wealth. Millions of individuals possess substantial assets, liquidity, and financial strength, yet find themselves constrained by outdated underwriting methods that fail to recognize the true depth of their financial position. This is where asset-based mortgage refinancing and equity access redefine what is possible. This book represents a turning point—not just in how you view mortgage lending, but in how you unlock the power of the wealth you have already built.

Asset-based mortgage refinancing is not simply about replacing one loan with another. It is about transforming dormant equity into active financial leverage. It is about converting illiquid wealth into opportunity without disrupting your long-term investment strategy. Whether you are holding significant funds in brokerage accounts, retirement portfolios, or other liquid assets, the ability to access that capital through refinancing opens doors that traditional income-based lending often keeps closed. In a world where flexibility, speed, and strategic positioning matter more than ever, understanding how to leverage your assets for liquidity is no longer optional—it is essential.

Throughout the previous books in this series, you have developed a foundation rooted in understanding how assets can replace income as the primary qualifying factor. You have learned how to structure approvals, navigate different borrower profiles, and position financial strength in a way that aligns with lender expectations. Now, in this ninth installment, we take that knowledge to the next level by focusing on one of the most powerful applications of asset-based lending: refinancing and equity extraction. This is where theory becomes transformation. This is where your existing real estate portfolio begins to work for you in ways that extend far beyond simple ownership.

Refinancing with an asset-based approach allows you to break free from the limitations of tax returns, employment verification, and income ratios that often fail to reflect real financial capability. Instead of asking, "How much do you earn?" the question becomes, "What resources do you control, and how can they be structured effectively?" This shift changes everything. It enables borrowers to access capital even during periods of reduced or unconventional income. It empowers retirees, entrepreneurs, investors, and high-net-worth individuals to tap into their equity without compromising their financial identity. It provides a pathway to liquidity that aligns with how modern wealth is actually built and maintained.

Equity, in its simplest form, represents ownership. But in practical terms, it represents potential—potential that is often underutilized. Many property owners accumulate significant equity over time, only to leave it untouched due to uncertainty, complexity, or fear of navigating the lending process. This book is designed to eliminate that uncertainty. It will show you how to view your equity not as a static number, but as a dynamic tool that can be strategically deployed to create new opportunities. Whether your goal is to reinvest in additional properties, consolidate debt, fund business ventures, or simply increase liquidity, asset-based refinancing provides a framework to make it happen.

One of the most powerful aspects of asset-based refinancing is its ability to align with long-term wealth strategies. Traditional cash-out refinancing often forces borrowers into rigid structures that may not align with their broader financial goals. In contrast, asset-based approaches allow for more nuanced structuring. You can maintain investment positions, avoid unnecessary asset liquidation, and preserve the growth potential of your portfolio while still accessing the capital you need. This balance between liquidity and preservation is what makes asset-based lending such a compelling strategy for sophisticated borrowers.

As you move through this book, you will begin to see refinancing not as a reactive decision, but as a proactive strategy. Instead of waiting for rates to drop or circumstances to force a change, you will learn how to evaluate your financial position and identify opportunities to optimize it. You will understand when it makes sense to extract equity, how much to leverage, and how to structure your loan in a way that supports both short-term objectives and long-term growth. This level of control transforms refinancing from a transactional event into a strategic advantage.

Another critical dimension of asset-based equity access is speed and adaptability. In competitive markets, timing can determine whether an opportunity is captured or missed. Traditional lending processes, with their extensive documentation requirements and rigid guidelines, can slow borrowers down at precisely the moment they need to act quickly. Asset-based lending, when properly structured, offers a more streamlined path to approval. By focusing on assets rather than income, lenders can evaluate risk more efficiently, allowing borrowers to access funds in a timeframe that aligns with real-world opportunities. It is also important to recognize that asset-based refinancing is not limited to a single borrower profile. While it is often associated with high-net-worth individuals, its applications extend far beyond that category. Entrepreneurs with fluctuating income, retirees living off investment distributions, self-employed professionals, and real estate investors all stand to benefit from this approach. The common thread is not income—it is the presence of assets and the ability to position them effectively. This book will guide you through the nuances of different borrower scenarios, helping you understand how asset-based strategies can be tailored to meet a wide range of financial situations.

Risk management is another essential component of this conversation. Accessing equity and increasing leverage must be approached with clarity and discipline. The goal is not simply to extract as much capital as possible, but to do so in a way that enhances your overall financial position. This requires an understanding of loan-to-value ratios, asset depletion methodologies, reserve requirements, and market dynamics. It requires a strategic mindset that balances opportunity with responsibility. Throughout this book, you will learn how to evaluate these factors and make informed decisions that support sustainable growth.

In addition to the technical aspects of asset-based refinancing, this book will also address the psychological shift required to fully embrace this strategy. Many borrowers are conditioned to view debt as something to be minimized or avoided. While this perspective has its place, it can also limit the ability to use leverage effectively. When structured properly, debt becomes a tool—a means of amplifying opportunity rather than restricting it. Asset-based refinancing reframes this relationship, showing you how to use leverage intelligently while maintaining control and flexibility.

You will also explore how different types of assets are evaluated in the refinancing process. Not all assets are treated equally, and understanding how lenders view liquidity, volatility, and accessibility is key to structuring a successful loan. From cash and brokerage accounts to retirement funds and alternative investments, each asset category carries its own considerations. This book will break down these distinctions, providing clarity on how to present your financial profile in the strongest possible light.

Another key focus will be the integration of asset-based refinancing into broader investment strategies. For real estate investors, this may involve using extracted equity to acquire additional properties, thereby accelerating portfolio growth. For business owners, it may mean funding expansion without disrupting operational cash flow. For individuals seeking financial flexibility, it may provide a safety net that enhances peace of mind. Regardless of your specific goals, the ability to access equity on your terms creates a level of control that is difficult to achieve through traditional financing methods.

As you progress through the chapters ahead, you will gain a comprehensive understanding of how to navigate the asset-based refinancing landscape. You will learn how to prepare your financial profile, select the right loan structures, and work with lenders who understand the value of asset-driven qualification. You will see real-world examples that illustrate both the opportunities and the challenges of this approach. Most importantly, you will develop the confidence to take action, knowing that you have the knowledge and framework to make informed decisions.

This book is not just about accessing equity—it is about unlocking potential. It is about recognizing that the wealth you have built is not static, but dynamic, and that with the right strategies, it can be leveraged to create even greater opportunities. It is about moving beyond the limitations of traditional lending and embracing a model that reflects the realities of modern finance. In doing so, you position yourself not just as a borrower, but as a strategist—someone who understands how to use every available resource to achieve their goals. By the time you reach the end of this book, you will no longer see refinancing as a complex or intimidating process. Instead, you will see it as a powerful tool—one that, when used correctly, can transform your financial trajectory. You will understand how to access liquidity without sacrificing growth, how to structure loans that align with your objectives, and how to navigate the lending landscape with confidence. This is the essence of asset-based mortgage refinancing and equity access. This is where your assets begin to work for you in a deeper, more strategic way.

Chapter 1

Understanding Asset-Based Refinancing and Equity Access

Asset-based refinancing begins with a fundamental shift in perspective: your assets are not just a reflection of your wealth—they are a source of usable power. Traditional mortgage refinancing evaluates borrowers primarily through income, employment stability, and debt-to-income ratios. However, asset-based refinancing reframes the entire process by focusing on what you already own and how those assets can support your ability to repay a loan. This approach is especially powerful for individuals whose financial strength lies in accumulated wealth rather than predictable monthly income. In this chapter, you will develop a deep understanding of how asset-based refinancing works, why it is increasingly relevant in today's financial environment, and how to position yourself to take full advantage of it.

At its core, refinancing is the process of replacing an existing mortgage with a new one. This can be done to secure better terms, reduce interest rates, extend or shorten loan duration, or access equity through a cash-out refinance. In the traditional system, borrowers must demonstrate sufficient income to qualify for the new loan. This creates a barrier for many individuals who may have significant assets but limited reportable income, such as retirees, business owners who reinvest profits, or investors whose income fluctuates. Asset-based refinancing removes this barrier by allowing lenders to evaluate your assets as the primary source of repayment capacity.

The key mechanism behind asset-based refinancing is known as asset depletion or asset utilization. Instead of relying on income, lenders calculate a theoretical monthly income based on the borrower's assets. This is typically done by dividing the total eligible assets over a set period, such as 60, 120, or 360 months, depending on the lender and program. The result is a calculated monthly figure that represents your ability to service debt. This figure is then used in place of traditional income when determining loan eligibility. The elegance of this approach lies in its simplicity: it translates wealth into cash flow without requiring liquidation.

Understanding which assets qualify is essential. Not all assets are treated equally in the underwriting process. Liquid assets such as cash, checking and savings accounts, and publicly traded securities are generally given the highest value because they are easily accessible and can be converted into cash quickly. Retirement accounts such as 401(k)s and IRAs are also commonly included, although they may be discounted to account for potential penalties and taxes. Other assets, such as business ownership stakes or illiquid investments, may be considered on a case-by-case basis, depending on the lender's guidelines. The goal is to create a clear and realistic picture of your financial capacity without overstating risk.

Another critical concept is loan-to-value ratio, or LTV. This metric represents the relationship between the loan amount and the value of the property. In a cash-out refinance, the lender will determine how much equity you can access based on a maximum allowable LTV. For example, if your property is worth $1,000,000 and the maximum LTV is 70%, the total loan amount cannot exceed $700,000. If your current loan balance is $400,000, this means you may be able to access up to $300,000 in equity. Asset-based refinancing works within these same structural limits, but the difference lies in how you qualify for the loan.

One of the most powerful advantages of asset-based refinancing is the ability to maintain your investment portfolio while accessing liquidity. In traditional scenarios, borrowers may be forced to sell assets to generate cash, potentially triggering taxes, fees, or lost growth opportunities. With asset-based refinancing, you can leverage your assets without liquidating them. This allows your investments to continue compounding while you simultaneously access the capital you need. It is a strategy that aligns liquidity with long-term wealth preservation.

Risk assessment in asset-based refinancing is also unique. Lenders are less concerned with employment history and more focused on the stability and composition of your asset base. A diversified portfolio with a strong balance of liquid and semi-liquid assets is viewed more favorably than concentrated or highly volatile holdings. This means that how your assets are structured can significantly impact your approval and loan terms. Borrowers who understand this can proactively position themselves to present a stronger financial profile.

Timing is another important factor. Refinancing decisions should not be made solely based on interest rates, although rates do play a role. Instead, asset-based refinancing should be viewed as part of a broader financial strategy. The question is not just whether you can refinance, but whether doing so advances your overall objectives. Are you using the funds to acquire additional income-producing assets? Are you consolidating higher-interest debt? Are you creating a liquidity buffer for future opportunities? When refinancing is aligned with a clear purpose, it becomes a tool for growth rather than just a financial adjustment. The role of reserves is also critical in asset-based lending. Lenders typically require borrowers to maintain a certain level of post-closing reserves, often measured in months of mortgage payments. These reserves provide an additional layer of security and demonstrate that the borrower has sufficient resources to manage the loan over time. In asset-based refinancing, reserves are often easier to satisfy because the borrower's qualification is already rooted in their asset base. However, understanding these requirements is essential to avoid surprises during the approval process.

Another dimension to consider is the type of refinance structure. Cash-out refinancing is the most common form of equity access, but it is not the only option. Rate-and-term refinancing, which adjusts the interest rate or loan duration without extracting cash, can also be approached through asset-based qualification. This can be particularly useful for borrowers who want to improve their loan terms without altering their liquidity position. Additionally, hybrid strategies can be used to balance both objectives, providing partial cash access while optimizing loan conditions.

As you move deeper into asset-based refinancing, you begin to see that it is not just a financial product—it is a strategic framework. It allows you to think differently about how your wealth is utilized. Instead of viewing assets as static holdings, you begin to see them as dynamic tools that can be leveraged to create new opportunities. This shift in mindset is what separates passive ownership from active financial strategy.

The modern financial environment continues to evolve, and with it, the tools available to borrowers. Asset-based refinancing represents a response to this evolution. It acknowledges that wealth is no longer defined solely by income, and that financial capability can take many forms. For those who understand how to navigate this system, the rewards can be significant. Increased liquidity, enhanced flexibility, and the ability to act quickly on opportunities are just a few of the benefits.

Ultimately, the goal of this chapter is to provide you with a clear and comprehensive foundation. By understanding how asset-based refinancing works, what factors influence approval, and how to position your assets effectively, you are preparing yourself to take advantage of one of the most powerful tools in modern lending. The chapters that follow will build on this foundation, exploring advanced strategies, real-world applications, and practical steps to implement what you have learned.

Real-Life Math Example: Asset-Based Cash-Out Refinance Strategy

Consider a real-world scenario involving a borrower named Daniel, a 52-year-old investor who owns a primary residence and several investment accounts. Daniel's home is currently valued at $1,200,000, and he has an existing mortgage balance of $450,000. His goal is to access equity from his home to invest in additional real estate opportunities without selling his existing assets. However, Daniel's reported income is relatively low because he reinvests most of his earnings back into his portfolio. This makes traditional refinancing difficult, but asset-based refinancing provides a solution.

Daniel's financial profile includes $800,000 in a brokerage account, $600,000 in a retirement account, and $100,000 in cash reserves. The lender evaluates these assets and applies standard guidelines. The brokerage account is considered fully eligible, while the retirement account is discounted by 30% to account for potential taxes and penalties, resulting in an adjusted value of $420,000. Combined with his cash reserves, Daniel's total eligible assets are calculated as $800,000 + $420,000 + $100,000 = $1,320,000.

The lender then applies an asset depletion formula over 120 months. This means Daniel's assets are divided by 120 to determine a monthly income equivalent. The calculation is $1,320,000 ÷ 120 = $11,000 per month. This figure becomes Daniel's qualifying income for the purposes of underwriting. Despite having limited traditional income, Daniel now appears as a strong borrower with substantial repayment capacity. Next, the lender evaluates the property's value and determines the maximum allowable loan based on a 70% LTV. With a property value of $1,200,000, the maximum loan amount is $840,000. Subtracting Daniel's existing mortgage balance of $450,000, the available cash-out amount is $390,000. This represents the equity Daniel can access through refinancing.

The new loan is structured at $840,000 with a 30-year term and a fixed interest rate of 6.5%. Daniel's estimated monthly payment, including principal and interest, is approximately $5,300. When compared to his calculated asset-based income of $11,000 per month, his housing ratio is well within acceptable limits. Additionally, Daniel is required to maintain 12 months of reserves, which equates to approximately $63,600. Given his asset base, this requirement is easily satisfied.

With $390,000 in cash-out proceeds, Daniel decides to allocate $300,000 toward the purchase of a new investment property and retains $90,000 as additional liquidity. The new property generates rental income, which further strengthens his financial position. Importantly, Daniel achieves this without liquidating his existing investments, allowing his portfolio to continue growing.

Over time, the benefits of this strategy compound. Daniel now controls a larger real estate portfolio, has increased cash flow from rental income, and maintains a strong asset base. The refinancing has effectively transformed his existing equity into a catalyst for expansion. By using asset-based qualification, he bypassed the limitations of traditional income verification and leveraged his true financial strength.

This example illustrates the power of asset-based refinancing when applied strategically. It demonstrates how assets can be converted into qualifying income, how equity can be accessed within LTV constraints, and how the resulting capital can be deployed to create new opportunities. For borrowers who understand these principles, the possibilities extend far beyond a single transaction. It becomes a repeatable system for growth, liquidity, and long-term wealth building.

Chapter 2

Structuring the Perfect Asset-Based Cash-Out Refinance

Asset-based refinancing is not just about qualifying—it is about structuring. The difference between an average refinance and a powerful wealth-building move lies in how the loan is designed, how the assets are positioned, and how the extracted equity is deployed. In this chapter, you will learn how to structure an asset-based cash-out refinance with precision, ensuring that every element of the transaction aligns with your long-term financial goals. This is where strategy replaces guesswork, and where thoughtful planning turns a simple refinance into a scalable financial system.

The first step in structuring the perfect asset-based refinance is clarity of purpose. Before any numbers are calculated or documents are submitted, you must define exactly why you are accessing equity. This purpose drives every decision that follows. Are you extracting capital to acquire additional real estate, expand a business, eliminate high-interest debt, or create liquidity for future opportunities? Each objective requires a slightly different structure. For example, if your goal is investment expansion, you may prioritize maximizing cash-out while maintaining acceptable risk. If your goal is stability, you may focus on optimizing loan terms and minimizing payment obligations. Without clarity, even the best loan structure can become inefficient.

Once your objective is defined, the next step is determining the optimal loan-to-value ratio. While lenders set maximum LTV limits, the most effective borrowers rarely push to the absolute maximum unless it aligns with a specific strategy. Instead, they choose a leverage point that balances liquidity with long-term safety. For instance, accessing equity at 65% LTV instead of 70% may reduce risk exposure while still providing sufficient capital. This decision is not purely mathematical—it is strategic. It reflects your tolerance for leverage, your outlook on the market, and your confidence in how the funds will be used.

Asset positioning plays a central role in structuring. Not all assets are treated equally, and how they are presented can influence both approval and terms. A borrower with $1 million in diversified, liquid assets will typically receive more favorable consideration than a borrower with the same value concentrated in illiquid or volatile holdings. Therefore, one of the most overlooked strategies is pre-structuring your asset portfolio before applying. This may involve reallocating funds into more liquid accounts, consolidating assets for clarity, or ensuring that documentation clearly reflects ownership and accessibility. The goal is to present a financial profile that is both strong and easy for the lender to evaluate.

Another key factor is the asset depletion term selected by the lender. Some programs use 60 months, others 120 or even 360 months. A shorter depletion term results in higher calculated monthly income, which can support a larger loan amount. However, it may also come with stricter requirements or higher perceived risk. A longer term produces lower qualifying income but may offer more flexibility. Understanding how these terms impact your approval allows you to select the program that best aligns with your goals. This is not a one-size-fits-all decision—it is a strategic choice based on your financial profile.

Interest rate selection is another critical component. While many borrowers focus solely on obtaining the lowest possible rate, experienced borrowers understand that rate must be evaluated in context. A slightly higher rate may be acceptable if it allows for greater cash-out, fewer restrictions, or faster closing. Conversely, a lower rate may be preferable if the primary goal is long-term cost reduction. The key is to evaluate the total impact of the loan, not just a single variable. This includes considering points, fees, prepayment penalties, and overall flexibility.

Loan term selection further shapes the structure. A 30-year term offers lower monthly payments and greater cash flow flexibility, which can be advantageous for investors or those prioritizing liquidity. A 15- or 20-year term, on the other hand, accelerates equity buildup and reduces total interest paid over time. In asset-based refinancing, the choice of term should align with how you intend to use the funds. If the extracted equity is being deployed into higher-yield investments, a longer term may enhance overall returns. If the focus is on reducing debt, a shorter term may be more appropriate.

Reserves and post-closing liquidity must also be carefully planned. Lenders typically require a certain number of months of reserves, but beyond meeting the minimum, you should consider your own comfort level. Maintaining sufficient liquidity after closing ensures that you can handle unexpected expenses, market fluctuations, or new opportunities. One of the most common mistakes borrowers make is extracting maximum equity without leaving a buffer. A well-structured refinance always includes a margin of safety.

Another advanced consideration is layering strategies. Asset-based refinancing does not have to exist in isolation. It can be combined with other financial tools to enhance its effectiveness. For example, a borrower may use a cash-out refinance in conjunction with a home equity line of credit to create both immediate capital and ongoing access to funds. Alternatively, extracted equity can be paired with business credit or private financing to amplify purchasing power. These layered approaches require careful coordination, but they can significantly expand what is possible.

Tax implications should also be part of the structuring process. While mortgage interest may be deductible in certain cases, the use of funds can influence how those deductions apply. Additionally, avoiding the liquidation of assets can prevent capital gains taxes, which is one of the key advantages of asset-based refinancing. Working with a knowledgeable tax advisor can help ensure that your strategy is optimized from both a lending and tax perspective. This is particularly important for high-net-worth individuals and investors managing multiple income streams.

Market conditions add another layer of complexity. Interest rates, property values, and lending guidelines are constantly evolving. A well-structured refinance takes these factors into account. For example, in a rising rate environment, locking in a fixed rate may provide long-term stability. In a strong appreciation market, accessing equity earlier may allow you to deploy capital before conditions change. Timing is not about predicting the future perfectly—it is about positioning yourself advantageously based on current trends. Finally, execution is what brings the structure to life. This involves selecting the right lender, preparing documentation, and navigating the approval process efficiently. Not all lenders specialize in asset-based programs, and choosing the right one can make a significant difference in both experience and outcome. Clear communication, organized documentation, and proactive planning can reduce delays and increase the likelihood of a smooth closing. The structure you design is only as effective as your ability to execute it.

By the end of this chapter, you should understand that structuring an asset-based refinance is both an art and a science. It requires technical knowledge, strategic thinking, and a clear understanding of your goals. When done correctly, it transforms a simple loan into a powerful financial instrument—one that can be used repeatedly to build, protect, and expand your wealth.

Real-Life Math Example: Structuring a Strategic Asset-Based Cash-Out Refinance

Consider a borrower named Sophia, a 60-year-old semi-retired entrepreneur who owns a primary residence valued at $950,000. She has an existing mortgage balance of $300,000 and wants to access equity to fund a combination of real estate investments and personal liquidity. Sophia's reported income is minimal, as she primarily lives off her investment portfolio, making traditional refinancing difficult. Sophia's assets include $500,000 in a brokerage account, $400,000 in a retirement account, and $150,000 in cash. The lender evaluates these assets and applies standard adjustments. The brokerage account is fully eligible, the retirement account is discounted by 30% to $280,000, and the cash is fully counted. This results in total eligible assets of $500,000 + $280,000 + $150,000 = $930,000.

The lender offers two asset depletion options: 60 months or 120 months. Sophia chooses the 60-month option to maximize her qualifying income. The calculation is $930,000 ÷ 60 = $15,500 per month. This higher income figure allows her to qualify for a larger loan amount. Her decision reflects her strategy of prioritizing maximum leverage for investment purposes.

Next, the lender determines the maximum loan amount based on a 70% LTV. With a property value of $950,000, the maximum loan is $665,000. Subtracting her existing balance of $300,000, Sophia can access $365,000 in cash-out proceeds. However, instead of taking the full amount, she strategically chooses to limit her loan to $640,000, resulting in $340,000 in cash-out. This slightly lower LTV reduces her risk while still providing substantial capital.

The loan is structured as a 30-year fixed mortgage at an interest rate of 6.75%. Her monthly payment is approximately $4,150. With a calculated income of $15,500 per month, her housing ratio remains well within acceptable limits. The lender requires 12 months of reserves, which equates to roughly $50,000. Sophia easily meets this requirement with her remaining assets.

Sophia allocates her $340,000 strategically. She invests $250,000 into a rental property that generates $2,200 per month in income and retains $90,000 as liquidity. The rental income offsets a significant portion of her new mortgage payment, effectively reducing her net cost. Meanwhile, her remaining assets continue to grow, as she has not liquidated her investments.

Over the next several years, Sophia benefits from both property appreciation and rental income. The new investment property increases in value, and her equity position strengthens across both properties. Additionally, her liquidity provides flexibility to respond to new opportunities or market changes. By structuring her refinance thoughtfully, she has transformed her home equity into a productive asset without compromising her financial stability.

This example highlights the importance of strategic decision-making at every stage of the process. From selecting the asset depletion term to choosing the appropriate LTV and allocating funds effectively, each choice contributes to the overall success of the refinance. It demonstrates that asset-based refinancing is not just about accessing capital—it is about doing so in a way that enhances your financial position over time.

When you approach refinancing with this level of intention, you move beyond basic transactions and into the realm of financial engineering. You begin to see how each variable—assets, leverage, rates, and deployment—interacts to create outcomes. This is the essence of structuring the perfect asset-based cash-out refinance, and it is a skill that can be applied repeatedly as your portfolio grows.

Chapter 3

Maximizing Liquidity Without Sacrificing Long-Term Wealth

One of the most powerful advantages of asset-based mortgage refinancing is the ability to access liquidity without dismantling the very foundation of your wealth. Traditional financial strategies often force individuals into a difficult choice: sell assets to generate cash or preserve investments and remain illiquid. Asset-based refinancing eliminates this trade-off by allowing borrowers to unlock capital while keeping their portfolios intact. In this chapter, you will learn how to maximize liquidity strategically, ensuring that every dollar you access serves a purpose while your long-term wealth continues to grow.

Liquidity, in practical terms, is the ability to access cash quickly without disrupting your financial structure. It is the fuel that allows you to act on opportunities, navigate uncertainty, and maintain flexibility. However, liquidity that comes at the expense of long-term growth can be counterproductive. Selling appreciating assets, triggering taxes, and losing compounding potential can erode wealth over time. Asset-based refinancing offers a solution by converting equity and asset strength into usable capital without requiring liquidation. The key is understanding how to strike the right balance between access and preservation.

The first principle of maximizing liquidity is recognizing that not all capital is equal. The source of your liquidity matters. Cash generated from selling assets is fundamentally different from cash accessed through leverage. When you sell an asset, you permanently remove it from your portfolio and potentially incur taxes or fees. When you access liquidity through refinancing, you maintain ownership of your assets while gaining access to capital. This distinction is critical because it allows you to benefit from both liquidity and ongoing growth simultaneously.

Another essential concept is opportunity cost. Every financial decision carries an opportunity cost—the value of what you give up in order to pursue a particular action. In the context of asset-based refinancing, the opportunity cost of not accessing liquidity can be significant. Missed investment opportunities, delayed acquisitions, or inability to act during favorable market conditions can limit your growth. Conversely, accessing too much liquidity without a clear plan can increase risk and reduce efficiency. The goal is to calibrate your liquidity to match your strategic objectives. Asset-based refinancing allows you to create what can be described as "strategic liquidity." This is liquidity that is not just available, but intentionally aligned with your goals. For example, a real estate investor may use extracted equity to acquire additional properties that generate income and appreciation. A business owner may use liquidity to expand operations or invest in new ventures. Even individuals seeking financial security can benefit by creating a reserve that provides peace of mind and flexibility. In each case, liquidity is not idle—it is purposeful.

Maintaining your investment portfolio while accessing liquidity is one of the defining advantages of this approach. Investments, particularly those in diversified portfolios, benefit from time and compounding. Removing funds prematurely can disrupt this process and reduce long-term returns. By leveraging your assets instead of selling them, you allow your investments to continue working for you. This creates a dual effect: your portfolio grows while your extracted capital is deployed elsewhere. Over time, this can significantly amplify your overall wealth.

Risk management becomes increasingly important as you leverage assets to create liquidity. While borrowing against your equity provides access to capital, it also introduces obligations. Monthly payments, interest costs, and market fluctuations must all be considered. The key is to ensure that your liquidity strategy does not overextend your financial position. This involves maintaining reasonable loan-to-value ratios, preserving sufficient reserves, and ensuring that any deployed capital has a clear and realistic return potential.

Another critical factor is cash flow alignment. Liquidity strategies are most effective when they are supported by sustainable cash flow. For example, if you use a cash-out refinance to acquire a rental property, the income generated by that property can offset or even exceed your mortgage payment. This creates a self-sustaining cycle where your liquidity not only provides access to capital but also contributes to ongoing financial stability. Aligning liquidity with income-generating opportunities enhances both efficiency and security.

The concept of liquidity layering also plays a role in advanced strategies. Instead of relying on a single source of capital, sophisticated borrowers create multiple layers of liquidity. This may include a combination of cash reserves, asset-based refinancing, lines of credit, and investment income. By diversifying liquidity sources, you reduce reliance on any single mechanism and increase your ability to adapt to changing circumstances. This layered approach provides resilience and flexibility, particularly in uncertain markets.

Timing is another element that can influence the effectiveness of your liquidity strategy. Accessing liquidity during periods of strong property values and favorable lending conditions can maximize your available capital. Conversely, waiting too long may result in missed opportunities or less favorable terms. While it is impossible to predict market movements with certainty, understanding current conditions and acting strategically can significantly enhance outcomes.

Psychology also plays a role in how individuals approach liquidity. Many people are conditioned to avoid debt, viewing it as inherently negative. However, when used strategically, leverage becomes a tool for growth. The key is to shift from a mindset of avoidance to one of intentional use. This does not mean taking on unnecessary risk, but rather understanding how to use debt as a means of expanding opportunity. Asset-based refinancing provides a framework for doing this responsibly.

Another important consideration is the preservation of optionality. Liquidity provides choices. It allows you to act, to wait, to invest, or to protect. Without liquidity, even strong financial positions can become constrained. By maintaining access to capital, you retain the ability to respond to both opportunities and challenges. This flexibility is one of the most valuable aspects of asset-based refinancing, as it allows you to adapt without compromising your core financial structure.

As you integrate these principles, you begin to see liquidity not as a static resource, but as a dynamic component of your financial strategy. It is something that can be created, adjusted, and optimized over time. Asset-based refinancing becomes a tool for managing this process, allowing you to align your resources with your goals in a way that traditional methods cannot.

Ultimately, maximizing liquidity without sacrificing long-term wealth requires a balance of strategy, discipline, and foresight. It is about understanding the trade-offs, evaluating opportunities, and making decisions that support both immediate needs and future growth. When done correctly, it allows you to access the full potential of your financial position, creating a pathway to greater flexibility, resilience, and success.

Real-Life Math Example: Leveraging Liquidity While Preserving Investment Growth

Consider a borrower named Michael, a 55-year-old investor with a primary residence valued at $1,100,000 and an existing mortgage balance of $350,000. Michael has built a substantial investment portfolio consisting of $900,000 in a brokerage account, $500,000 in retirement funds, and $150,000 in cash. His goal is to access liquidity to invest in additional real estate while maintaining his existing portfolio and avoiding asset liquidation. The lender evaluates Michael's assets and applies standard adjustments. The brokerage account is fully eligible at $900,000. The retirement account is discounted by 30%, resulting in an adjusted value of $350,000. The cash is fully counted at $150,000. This gives Michael total eligible assets of $900,000 + $350,000 + $150,000 = $1,400,000.

The lender uses a 120-month asset depletion model to calculate Michael's qualifying income. The calculation is $1,400,000 ÷ 120 = $11,667 per month. This figure is used to determine his ability to support a new loan. Despite limited traditional income, Michael qualifies as a strong borrower based on his asset base.

Next, the lender determines the maximum loan amount based on a 70% LTV. With a property value of $1,100,000, the maximum loan is $770,000. Subtracting the existing mortgage balance of $350,000, Michael can access up to $420,000 in equity. However, to maintain a margin of safety, he chooses to refinance at $740,000, resulting in $390,000 in cash-out proceeds.

The new loan is structured as a 30-year fixed mortgage at an interest rate of 6.5%, with a monthly payment of approximately $4,680. Michael is required to maintain 12 months of reserves, totaling about $56,000, which he easily satisfies with his remaining assets.

Michael allocates his $390,000 strategically. He invests $300,000 into a rental property that generates $2,500 per month in income and retains $90,000 as additional liquidity. The rental income covers more than half of his new mortgage payment, effectively reducing his net out-of-pocket expense. Meanwhile, his original investment portfolio continues to grow, benefiting from market appreciation and compounding returns.

Over a five-year period, Michael's strategy produces multiple layers of growth. His brokerage account increases in value, his retirement funds continue to compound, and his new property appreciates while generating consistent income. The liquidity he accessed through refinancing has been transformed into an additional income-producing asset, enhancing both his cash flow and net worth.

If Michael had chosen to sell $390,000 of his investments instead, he would have faced potential capital gains taxes and lost future growth on those assets. By using asset-based refinancing instead, he preserved his portfolio while still achieving his investment goals. This illustrates the power of leveraging liquidity without sacrificing long-term wealth.

This example demonstrates how strategic liquidity can be created and deployed effectively. It shows how assets can be used to qualify for financing, how equity can be accessed within safe limits, and how the resulting capital can be invested to generate additional returns. It also highlights the importance of maintaining balance—ensuring that liquidity enhances, rather than compromises, financial stability.

When applied consistently, this approach becomes a repeatable system. Each cycle of refinancing, investing, and growth builds upon the previous one, creating momentum over time. This is the essence of maximizing liquidity through asset-based refinancing: using what you have to create what you want, without giving up what you have already built.

Chapter 4

Risk Management and Smart Leverage in Asset-Based Refinancing

Asset-based mortgage refinancing is one of the most powerful tools available for accessing liquidity and expanding wealth, but with that power comes responsibility. Leverage, when used correctly, can accelerate growth, increase opportunity, and enhance financial flexibility. When used incorrectly, it can magnify risk, reduce stability, and create long-term financial strain. The difference between success and failure in asset-based refinancing is not simply access to capital—it is how intelligently that capital is managed. In this chapter, you will learn how to apply disciplined risk management principles while using leverage to your advantage, ensuring that your strategy remains both aggressive enough to grow and conservative enough to endure.

The foundation of risk management begins with understanding leverage itself. Leverage is the use of borrowed capital to increase potential returns. In real estate, this typically involves using a loan to control a property or extract equity while maintaining ownership. Asset-based refinancing enhances this concept by allowing you to qualify based on your assets rather than your income. However, the presence of assets does not eliminate risk—it simply changes how it is evaluated. The key is to recognize that leverage amplifies both outcomes. Positive results can become greater, but negative outcomes can also become more severe if not properly managed.

One of the most important metrics in managing leverage is the loan-to-value ratio. LTV represents the percentage of the property's value that is financed through debt. Higher LTV ratios provide more immediate liquidity but increase exposure to market fluctuations. Lower LTV ratios provide greater stability and a stronger equity cushion. The decision of where to position your LTV is one of the most critical choices in asset-based refinancing. Conservative borrowers may choose to remain at or below 60–65% LTV to protect against market downturns, while more aggressive investors may operate closer to 70% or higher if the strategy justifies it. The key is alignment—your LTV should reflect your goals, your risk tolerance, and your overall financial position.

Another core component of risk management is cash flow stability. Regardless of how strong your asset base is, your ability to manage ongoing loan obligations depends on consistent cash flow. This can come from multiple sources, including rental income, investment distributions, business revenue, or reserves. A well-structured refinance ensures that your monthly obligations are sustainable under both normal and stressed conditions. This means evaluating not only your current cash flow, but also how it might change under different scenarios. For example, what happens if rental income decreases, markets fluctuate, or unexpected expenses arise? Planning for these possibilities strengthens your strategy.

Reserves act as a critical buffer against uncertainty. While lenders may require a minimum number of months of reserves, sophisticated borrowers often exceed these requirements. Maintaining 12 to 24 months of accessible liquidity can provide significant protection against unforeseen challenges. This reserve strategy ensures that you can continue to meet obligations without being forced to sell assets at unfavorable times. It also provides psychological confidence, allowing you to operate with clarity rather than fear.

Diversification is another essential principle. Relying on a single asset, income source, or investment strategy increases vulnerability. By spreading your financial exposure across multiple assets and income streams, you reduce the impact of any single adverse event. In the context of asset-based refinancing, diversification may involve holding a mix of real estate, securities, and cash, as well as deploying extracted equity across different opportunities rather than concentrating it in one area. This balanced approach enhances resilience and long-term sustainability. Interest rate risk is also a key consideration. The structure of your loan—whether fixed or adjustable—can significantly impact your financial position over time. Fixed-rate loans provide stability and predictability, making them ideal for long-term planning. Adjustable-rate loans may offer lower initial rates but introduce variability that must be carefully managed. Understanding how rate changes affect your payments and overall strategy is essential. In many cases, borrowers prioritize stability over short-term savings, particularly when managing significant leverage.

Market risk cannot be ignored. Real estate values, interest rates, and economic conditions are all subject to change. While it is impossible to predict market movements with certainty, you can prepare for them. This involves maintaining conservative assumptions, avoiding over-leverage, and ensuring that your strategy remains viable under less favorable conditions. For example, structuring a refinance in a way that remains sustainable even if property values decline or interest rates increase can protect your long-term position.

Another important concept is the purpose of leverage. Not all uses of borrowed capital are equal. Using equity to acquire income-producing assets or investments with strong return potential can enhance your financial position. Using leverage for non-productive purposes may provide short-term benefits but does not contribute to long-term growth. The most effective borrowers align their use of leverage with opportunities that generate returns, thereby creating a positive cycle of growth and reinvestment.

Psychological discipline is an often-overlooked aspect of risk management. The availability of liquidity can create a temptation to overextend. It is important to remain grounded in your strategy and avoid decisions driven by emotion or short-term thinking. This includes resisting the urge to maximize every refinance opportunity without considering long-term implications. Discipline ensures that your actions remain aligned with your goals and that your strategy remains sustainable.

Stress testing your strategy is another valuable practice. This involves evaluating how your financial position would perform under different scenarios. For example, what happens if interest rates increase by 1–2%, rental income decreases by 20%, or investment returns slow? By modeling these scenarios, you can identify potential weaknesses and adjust your strategy accordingly. This proactive approach allows you to prepare for challenges before they arise.

The concept of margin of safety ties all of these elements together. A margin of safety is the buffer between your current position and potential risk. It is created through conservative leverage, strong reserves, diversified assets, and disciplined decision-making. This margin allows you to absorb shocks without compromising your overall strategy. In asset-based refinancing, maintaining a margin of safety ensures that your use of leverage remains a tool for growth rather than a source of vulnerability.

Ultimately, risk management in asset-based refinancing is about balance. It is about using leverage to expand opportunity while maintaining control and stability. It is about understanding the interplay between assets, debt, and cash flow, and making decisions that support both immediate objectives and long-term success. When these principles are applied consistently, leverage becomes a powerful ally rather than a potential threat.

Real-Life Math Example: Managing Risk While Leveraging Equity

Consider a borrower named David, a 58-year-old investor with a primary residence valued at $1,300,000 and an existing mortgage balance of $500,000. David has accumulated a strong asset base, including $1,000,000 in a brokerage account, $600,000 in retirement funds, and $200,000 in cash. His goal is to access equity to invest in additional real estate while maintaining a conservative risk profile. The lender evaluates David's assets and applies standard adjustments. The brokerage account is fully eligible at $1,000,000. The retirement account is discounted by 30%, resulting in $420,000. The cash is fully counted at $200,000. This gives David total eligible assets of $1,000,000 + $420,000 + $200,000 = $1,620,000.

Using a 120-month asset depletion model, the lender calculates David's qualifying income as $1,620,000 ÷ 120 = $13,500 per month. This provides a strong income profile for underwriting purposes. However, David does not base his strategy solely on maximum qualification—he prioritizes risk management.

The lender allows a maximum LTV of 70%, which would permit a loan amount of $910,000. Subtracting his existing mortgage balance of $500,000, David could access $410,000 in equity. Instead of taking the full amount, David chooses a more conservative approach. He refinances at 65% LTV, resulting in a new loan of $845,000 and cash-out proceeds of $345,000. This decision reduces his leverage and increases his equity cushion.

The loan is structured as a 30-year fixed mortgage at 6.5%, resulting in a monthly payment of approximately $5,350. David ensures that he maintains 18 months of reserves, totaling around $96,000. This exceeds lender requirements and provides additional security. David allocates his $345,000 strategically. He invests $250,000 into a rental property that generates $2,400 per month and retains $95,000 as additional liquidity. The rental income covers a significant portion of his mortgage payment, reducing his net financial burden. Additionally, his remaining assets continue to grow, providing further stability.

David also stress-tests his strategy. He considers a scenario where rental income decreases by 20%, reducing it to $1,920 per month. Even under this condition, his overall cash flow remains manageable due to his reserves and diversified assets. He also evaluates the impact of potential market fluctuations and ensures that his equity position provides sufficient protection.

Over time, David benefits from both income generation and asset appreciation. His conservative leverage allows him to navigate market changes with confidence, while his strategic use of equity enhances his overall portfolio. By prioritizing risk management, he transforms asset-based refinancing into a sustainable growth strategy rather than a high-risk endeavor.

This example illustrates how disciplined decision-making can enhance the effectiveness of leverage. By choosing a lower

LTV, maintaining strong reserves, and aligning his investments with income generation, David creates a balanced and resilient financial position. His approach demonstrates that the true power of asset-based refinancing lies not just in access to capital, but in how that capital is managed.

When you apply these principles, you move beyond simply using leverage—you begin to control it. You create a system where risk is understood, managed, and aligned with opportunity. This is the foundation of long-term success in asset-based refinancing and equity access.

Chapter 5

Building a Repeatable Wealth System Using Asset-Based Refinancing

At this stage, you have learned how asset-based refinancing works, how to structure it effectively, how to maximize liquidity, and how to manage risk. Now, the next evolution is turning this knowledge into a repeatable system—one that can be used over and over again to build, expand, and compound wealth. The true power of asset-based refinancing is not in a single transaction. It is in its ability to be repeated strategically, creating a cycle of equity extraction, reinvestment, growth, and repositioning. This chapter is about building that system and understanding how to scale it intelligently over time.

A repeatable wealth system begins with a shift in mindset. Instead of viewing refinancing as a one-time event, you begin to see it as part of an ongoing process. Each property you own, each asset you accumulate, and each decision you make contributes to a larger financial engine. This engine is fueled by equity, liquidity, and strategic deployment. When properly designed, it allows you to continuously convert passive equity into active opportunity while maintaining control over your overall financial position. The foundation of this system is equity growth. Equity increases through two primary mechanisms: principal paydown and appreciation. Over time, as you make mortgage payments, your loan balance decreases, increasing your ownership stake in the property. Simultaneously, market appreciation can increase the property's value, further expanding your equity. Asset-based refinancing allows you to capture a portion of this equity without selling the property, turning it into usable capital. This creates the first stage of the cycle: equity extraction.

Once equity is extracted, the next stage is deployment. This is where many borrowers either accelerate their growth or limit their potential. The capital you access must be used intentionally. Ideally, it should be deployed into opportunities that generate returns—whether through income, appreciation, or both. Real estate is a common choice because it aligns well with leverage, but other investments may also be appropriate depending on your strategy. The key is that the capital should work for you, not sit idle.

As your deployed capital begins to generate returns, your financial position strengthens. Rental income, business profits, or investment gains contribute to your overall cash flow and asset base. This growth feeds back into the system, increasing your ability to qualify for future refinancing and expanding your available opportunities. This is the compounding effect of a well-designed system—each cycle builds upon the previous one.

Repositioning is another critical component of the system. Over time, your financial situation, market conditions, and goals will evolve. Asset-based refinancing allows you to adjust your strategy accordingly. This may involve refinancing existing properties to access additional equity, consolidating loans to improve terms, or reallocating capital to more productive opportunities. Repositioning ensures that your system remains dynamic and responsive rather than static and rigid.

Timing plays a significant role in this process. While it is not necessary to refinance constantly, identifying the right moments to act can significantly enhance your results. These moments may be driven by increases in property value, changes in interest rates, or new investment opportunities. By staying aware of these factors, you can position yourself to act when conditions are favorable, maximizing the effectiveness of each cycle.

Another important aspect of a repeatable system is scalability. As your portfolio grows, so does your ability to leverage it. However, scaling requires discipline. It is not simply about acquiring more properties or accessing more capital—it is about maintaining balance. Each new layer of leverage must be supported by sufficient cash flow, reserves, and risk management. Scaling too quickly without proper structure can create instability, while scaling strategically can lead to exponential growth.

The concept of velocity is also relevant. Velocity refers to how quickly you can move through each cycle of equity extraction and reinvestment. Faster cycles can accelerate growth, but they must be managed carefully to avoid overextension. The goal is not speed for its own sake, but efficiency. Each cycle should be executed with clarity, ensuring that the outcomes support your long-term objectives.

Tax efficiency is another factor that enhances the system. By accessing equity through refinancing rather than selling assets, you may avoid triggering capital gains taxes. Additionally, interest expenses may be deductible in certain situations, depending on how the funds are used. These advantages can improve your overall returns and allow more of your capital to remain invested. Integrating tax considerations into your strategy ensures that your system operates at maximum efficiency.

Diversification within the system provides stability. While real estate may serve as the core, incorporating other asset classes can reduce risk and enhance resilience. This might include maintaining a portion of your portfolio in liquid investments, holding different types of properties, or exploring complementary opportunities. Diversification ensures that your system can withstand changes in any single market or sector.

Another key element is tracking and measurement. A repeatable system must be monitored to ensure that it is performing as intended. This includes tracking metrics such as cash flow, equity growth, loan balances, and return on investment. By regularly reviewing these metrics, you can identify areas for improvement and make adjustments as needed. This level of awareness transforms your strategy from reactive to proactive.

Psychological consistency is also essential. Building a repeatable system requires patience and discipline. There will be periods of rapid growth and periods of slower progress. Staying committed to your strategy, rather than reacting emotionally to short-term fluctuations, ensures that your system remains intact. Consistency is what allows compounding to take effect over time.

Ultimately, the goal of this chapter is to help you see the bigger picture. Asset-based refinancing is not just a tool—it is a framework for building and scaling wealth. When integrated into a repeatable system, it allows you to continuously unlock and redeploy your resources, creating a cycle of growth that becomes more powerful with each iteration. This is how individuals move from isolated transactions to sustained financial expansion.

Real-Life Math Example: Building a Repeatable Refinancing System

Consider a borrower named Laura, a 50-year-old investor who begins with a single primary residence valued at $900,000 and a mortgage balance of $300,000. Laura also has $700,000 in a brokerage account and $200,000 in retirement funds. Her goal is to build a portfolio of income-producing properties using asset-based refinancing as her primary tool.

In the first cycle, Laura refinances her home at a 70% LTV. The maximum loan amount is $630,000. After paying off her existing mortgage of $300,000, she accesses $330,000 in cash. Her assets are evaluated, and her qualifying income is calculated using a 120-month depletion model. Her total eligible assets are $700,000 plus $140,000 (after discounting her retirement funds), resulting in $840,000. Divided over 120 months, her qualifying income is $7,000 per month, which supports her new loan.

Laura uses $250,000 of her cash-out proceeds to purchase a rental property that generates $2,200 per month in income. She retains $80,000 as reserves. Over the next three years, the property appreciates to $350,000, and her loan balance decreases slightly through payments.

In the second cycle, Laura refinances the rental property at 70% LTV. The new loan amount is $245,000. After paying off the existing balance of $200,000, she accesses $45,000 in additional equity. Combined with savings and accumulated cash flow, she uses this capital to acquire another property.

Simultaneously, her primary residence appreciates to $1,050,000. She performs another refinance, accessing additional equity while maintaining a manageable LTV. This provides her with another $100,000 in capital, which she uses as a down payment for a third property.

By the third cycle, Laura owns three properties generating a combined rental income of $6,000 per month. Her portfolio value has increased significantly, and her equity position continues to grow. Each property contributes to her overall financial strength, allowing her to qualify for further refinancing and expansion.

Over a ten-year period, Laura repeats this process multiple times. Each cycle builds on the previous one, increasing her portfolio size, cash flow, and net worth. Importantly, she maintains disciplined leverage, sufficient reserves, and diversified investments, ensuring that her system remains stable. If Laura had relied solely on saving income or selling assets, her growth would have been significantly slower. By using asset-based refinancing as a repeatable system, she accelerates her progress while maintaining control over her financial position. Her strategy demonstrates how equity can be continuously recycled into new opportunities, creating a compounding effect over time.

This example illustrates the power of repetition. Each refinance, each investment, and each cycle contributes to a larger system that becomes more efficient and effective as it grows. It shows that wealth is not built through isolated actions, but through consistent application of a well-designed strategy.

When you adopt this approach, you move beyond individual transactions and into a scalable model of financial growth. You begin to see how each decision fits into a broader system, and how that system can be refined and expanded over time. This is the essence of building a repeatable wealth system using asset-based refinancing—a process that transforms potential into performance and strategy into results.

Chapter 6

Timing the Market and Positioning for Maximum Equity Extraction

One of the most misunderstood aspects of asset-based mortgage refinancing is timing. Many borrowers wait passively, hoping for the "perfect" moment—typically defined by the lowest possible interest rates—before taking action. However, sophisticated borrowers understand that timing is not about perfection; it is about positioning. The ability to recognize favorable conditions, align them with your financial goals, and act decisively is what separates average outcomes from exceptional ones. In this chapter, you will learn how to evaluate market conditions, identify optimal refinance windows, and position yourself to extract maximum equity while maintaining strategic control.

Timing begins with understanding the three core drivers that influence refinancing opportunities: property values, interest rates, and lending guidelines. Property values determine how much equity is available. Interest rates influence the cost of borrowing. Lending guidelines dictate how easily you can qualify and how much flexibility you have in structuring your loan. These three factors are constantly shifting, and their interaction creates windows of opportunity. The goal is not to predict each movement perfectly, but to recognize when conditions align in your favor.

Property appreciation is often the most significant driver of equity growth. As property values increase, your available equity expands, creating opportunities for refinancing. However, appreciation does not occur in a straight line. Markets move in cycles, influenced by supply, demand, economic conditions, and local factors. Understanding these cycles allows you to anticipate periods of growth and act before the market stabilizes or declines. For example, refinancing during a strong appreciation phase can allow you to capture increased equity before values plateau.

Interest rates, while important, should be viewed in context rather than isolation. A common mistake is waiting indefinitely for rates to drop, only to miss opportunities created by rising property values or favorable lending conditions. In some cases, a slightly higher interest rate may be justified if it allows you to access significantly more equity or deploy capital into high-return opportunities. The key is to evaluate the total financial impact, not just the rate itself. Strategic borrowers focus on net outcomes rather than individual variables.

Lending guidelines also play a crucial role in timing. Asset-based programs, loan-to-value limits, reserve requirements, and documentation standards can change over time. Periods of more flexible lending can provide opportunities to structure deals that may not be available later. Staying informed about these changes allows you to act proactively rather than reactively. Working with lenders who specialize in asset-based financing can provide valuable insight into current and upcoming program shifts.

Positioning is what allows you to take advantage of timing. This involves preparing your financial profile in advance so that you are ready to act when opportunities arise. Positioning includes maintaining organized documentation, ensuring that your assets are clearly structured, and keeping your credit profile strong. It also involves monitoring your property values and understanding your current equity position. When you are properly positioned, you can move quickly and efficiently when the right moment presents itself.

Another important concept is equity harvesting. This refers to the process of extracting equity at strategic intervals rather than waiting for a single large event. By harvesting equity periodically, you can continuously deploy capital into new opportunities while maintaining control over your leverage. This approach aligns with the concept of a repeatable system, allowing you to build momentum over time rather than relying on a single transaction.

Market cycles create both opportunities and risks. During periods of rapid appreciation, it may be tempting to maximize leverage and extract as much equity as possible. While this can accelerate growth, it also increases exposure to potential downturns. Conversely, during periods of slower growth or uncertainty, maintaining a more conservative approach may provide greater stability. Understanding where you are in the market cycle allows you to adjust your strategy accordingly, balancing growth with protection.

Another layer of timing involves personal financial readiness. Even if market conditions are favorable, your ability to act depends on your own financial position. This includes having sufficient reserves, a clear strategy for deploying capital, and confidence in your ability to manage the resulting obligations. Timing is not just external—it is internal. The best opportunities occur when market conditions and personal readiness align.

Speed of execution is also critical. In competitive environments, delays can result in missed opportunities. Asset-based refinancing often provides an advantage in this area due to its streamlined approach to qualification. By focusing on assets rather than income, lenders can process applications more efficiently. However, this advantage is only realized if you are prepared. Having your documentation ready, understanding your strategy, and working with experienced professionals can significantly reduce closing times.

Another important concept is forward positioning. This involves anticipating future opportunities and preparing for them in advance. For example, if you expect property values to increase in a particular area, you may position yourself to refinance once that appreciation materializes. Similarly, if you anticipate changes in lending guidelines, you may act before those changes take effect. Forward positioning requires awareness, planning, and a willingness to act proactively.

The interplay between timing and leverage is also significant. Extracting equity at the right time can enhance your returns, while doing so at the wrong time can increase risk. For example, accessing equity at the peak of a market without a clear deployment strategy may expose you to unnecessary risk. Conversely, accessing equity during a growth phase and deploying it into strong opportunities can amplify your results. The goal is to align your leverage with both market conditions and your strategic objectives.

Psychological discipline plays a role here as well. Markets can create emotional responses—fear during downturns and overconfidence during upswings. Maintaining a disciplined approach ensures that your decisions are based on strategy rather than emotion. This includes sticking to your predetermined criteria for refinancing, rather than reacting impulsively to market movements.

Ultimately, timing and positioning are about creating advantage. They allow you to act when others hesitate, to capture opportunities that others miss, and to structure your financial moves with precision. Asset-based refinancing provides the flexibility to do this, but it requires awareness and preparation. When you combine these elements, you gain the ability to extract equity at the right moments and deploy it effectively, creating a powerful cycle of growth.

Real-Life Math Example: Timing Equity Extraction for Maximum Impact

Consider a borrower named Anthony, a 54-year-old investor who owns a primary residence initially valued at $800,000 with a mortgage balance of $250,000. Anthony also holds $600,000 in a brokerage account and $200,000 in retirement funds. His goal is to use asset-based refinancing to expand his real estate portfolio, but he wants to time his actions strategically to maximize his results.

In year one, Anthony observes that his local market is experiencing steady appreciation, with property values increasing by approximately 8% annually. Instead of refinancing immediately, he chooses to wait and monitor the trend. By the end of year two, his property value has increased to approximately $933,000. This appreciation significantly increases his available equity.

At this point, Anthony decides to act. The lender allows a maximum LTV of 70%, which translates to a potential loan amount of $653,100. After paying off his existing mortgage of $250,000, Anthony can access $403,100 in equity. His assets are evaluated, with his brokerage account fully counted and his retirement account discounted to $140,000, resulting in total eligible assets of $740,000. Using a 120-month depletion model, his qualifying income is calculated at approximately $6,167 per month.

Anthony structures his refinance at $640,000, slightly below the maximum, resulting in $390,000 in cash-out proceeds. His new loan carries a 6.5% interest rate with a monthly payment of approximately $4,050. He maintains sufficient reserves to meet and exceed lender requirements.

Anthony deploys his capital strategically. He invests $300,000 into a rental property that generates $2,300 per month and retains $90,000 as liquidity. Over the next two years, both his primary residence and investment property continue to appreciate. The new property increases in value to $380,000, while his primary residence reaches $1,020,000. At this stage, Anthony evaluates the market again. Interest rates have increased slightly, but property values remain strong. He decides to perform a second refinance on his primary residence. At a 65% LTV, he accesses an additional $60,000 in equity. Combined with accumulated cash flow, he uses this capital as a down payment for another investment property.

By year five, Anthony owns three properties with a combined value exceeding $1.6 million. His rental income covers a significant portion of his mortgage obligations, and his asset base has grown substantially. Importantly, his success is not the result of a single refinance, but of carefully timed actions aligned with market conditions.

If Anthony had refinanced in year one, he would have accessed significantly less equity due to lower property values. If he had waited too long, he might have faced less favorable lending conditions or missed opportunities. By timing his actions strategically, he maximized both his equity extraction and his ability to deploy capital effectively.

This example demonstrates how timing and positioning work

together to enhance outcomes. It shows how monitoring market conditions, waiting for appreciation, and acting decisively can create significant advantages. It also highlights the importance of balancing patience with action—waiting for the right moment, but not waiting indefinitely.

When you apply these principles, you begin to see refinancing not as a reactive decision, but as a strategic move within a larger system. You gain the ability to align your actions with market conditions, optimize your results, and build momentum over time. This is the essence of timing the market and positioning for maximum equity extraction—a skill that can significantly amplify your success in asset-based refinancing.

Chapter 7

Advanced Strategies for Scaling Portfolio Growth with Asset-Based Refinancing

As you progress deeper into asset-based mortgage refinancing, you begin to realize that the true potential of this strategy lies not in isolated transactions, but in scaling. Scaling is the process of expanding your portfolio, increasing your income streams, and amplifying your net worth in a structured and sustainable way. It requires more than just access to capital—it requires coordination, sequencing, and strategic layering of financial decisions. In this chapter, you will learn advanced strategies for scaling your portfolio using asset-based refinancing, allowing you to move from incremental growth to exponential expansion.

The first principle of scaling is understanding leverage stacking. Leverage stacking involves using multiple layers of financing and capital sources to maximize your purchasing power. Asset-based refinancing provides the initial layer by unlocking equity from existing properties. This capital can then be combined with other financing tools, such as conventional loans, DSCR loans, private financing, or business credit, to acquire additional assets. The goal is to use each layer efficiently, ensuring that the combined structure enhances your overall position rather than overextending it.

Another key concept is portfolio compounding. As you acquire more properties, each one contributes to your overall financial ecosystem. Rental income increases your cash flow, appreciation increases your equity, and both factors enhance your ability to refinance and expand further. This creates a compounding effect where each new asset accelerates the growth of the entire portfolio. Asset-based refinancing plays a central role in this process by allowing you to continuously access and redeploy equity without disrupting your existing holdings.

Sequencing is critical in scaling. The order in which you execute transactions can significantly impact your results. For example, refinancing a primary residence to access capital may provide the funds needed to acquire an investment property. Once that property stabilizes and appreciates, it can be refinanced to fund additional acquisitions. This sequential approach ensures that each step builds on the previous one, creating a structured pathway for growth. Without proper sequencing, you may miss opportunities or create inefficiencies in your strategy. Cash flow optimization becomes increasingly important as your portfolio grows. Each property should contribute positively to your overall financial position. This does not necessarily mean that every property must generate immediate profit, but the portfolio as a whole should be sustainable. Asset-based refinancing allows you to structure loans in a way that supports this goal, whether through longer terms, interest-only periods, or strategic rate selection. The objective is to maintain flexibility while ensuring that your obligations remain manageable.

Another advanced strategy is equity recycling. This involves repeatedly extracting equity from your properties and reinvesting it into new opportunities. Equity recycling is the engine that drives portfolio expansion. However, it must be executed with discipline. Each cycle should be based on clear criteria, including property performance, market conditions, and your overall leverage position. By establishing a consistent framework for when and how to recycle equity, you create a repeatable process that can be scaled over time.

Diversification within your portfolio enhances both growth and stability. As you scale, consider expanding into different property types, locations, or investment strategies. This reduces reliance on any single market or asset class and provides multiple sources of income and appreciation. Asset-based refinancing supports diversification by providing flexible access to capital that can be deployed across a range of opportunities. Another important element is operational efficiency. Managing a growing portfolio requires systems and processes that can handle increased complexity. This includes property management, financial tracking, and decision-making frameworks. While asset-based refinancing provides the capital for growth, operational efficiency ensures that your portfolio remains organized and sustainable. As you scale, investing in systems and support can significantly enhance your ability to manage and expand your holdings.

Risk layering must also be carefully managed. As you add more properties and leverage, your exposure increases. Each layer of financing introduces additional obligations and potential risks. Understanding how these layers interact is essential. For example, ensuring that your overall debt structure remains balanced, maintaining sufficient reserves across your portfolio, and avoiding over-concentration in any single area are all critical to long-term success.

The concept of portfolio velocity becomes more relevant at this stage. Velocity refers to how quickly you can move from one stage of growth to the next. Higher velocity can accelerate your expansion, but it must be balanced with stability. Moving too quickly without proper structure can lead to inefficiencies or increased risk. The goal is to maintain a pace that allows for consistent growth while preserving control. Strategic partnerships can also enhance scaling efforts. Working with lenders, investors, or partners who understand asset-based financing can provide additional resources and opportunities. These relationships can help you access better terms, identify new deals, and execute transactions more efficiently. While not required, partnerships can significantly expand your capacity to scale.

Another advanced concept is portfolio optimization. As your portfolio grows, not all assets will perform equally. Some properties may appreciate more rapidly, generate higher income, or present better refinancing opportunities. Regularly evaluating your portfolio allows you to identify which assets should be leveraged further, which should be held, and which may be repositioned. This ongoing optimization ensures that your portfolio remains aligned with your goals.

Long-term vision is what ties all of these strategies together. Scaling is not just about acquiring more assets—it is about building a financial structure that supports your desired lifestyle and objectives. Whether your goal is financial independence, generational wealth, or business expansion, your portfolio should be designed to support that vision. Asset-based refinancing provides the flexibility to adapt and evolve as your goals change. Ultimately, scaling through asset-based refinancing is about creating momentum. Each decision, each transaction, and each cycle contributes to a larger system that becomes more powerful over time. When executed with strategy and discipline, this approach allows you to move beyond incremental growth and into a phase of accelerated expansion.

Real-Life Math Example: Scaling a Portfolio Using Asset-Based Refinancing

Consider a borrower named Carlos, a 48-year-old investor who begins with a primary residence valued at $850,000 and a mortgage balance of $250,000. Carlos also has $500,000 in a brokerage account and $150,000 in retirement funds. His goal is to build a portfolio of income-producing properties using asset-based refinancing as his primary growth strategy.

In the first stage, Carlos refinances his primary residence at a 70% LTV. The maximum loan amount is $595,000. After paying off his existing mortgage, he accesses $345,000 in cash. His assets are evaluated, with his brokerage account fully counted and his retirement account discounted to $105,000, resulting in total eligible assets of $605,000. Using a 120-month depletion model, his qualifying income is approximately $5,042 per month.

Carlos uses $250,000 of his cash-out proceeds to purchase his first rental property, which generates $2,100 per month in income. He retains $95,000 as reserves. Over the next two years, the property appreciates to $320,000, and Carlos benefits from both rental income and equity growth.

In the second stage, Carlos refinances the rental property at 70% LTV. The new loan amount is $224,000. After paying off the existing balance of $180,000, he accesses $44,000 in additional equity. Combined with savings and cash flow, he uses this capital as a down payment for a second rental property.

Simultaneously, his primary residence appreciates to $950,000. Carlos performs another refinance, accessing an additional $70,000 in equity while maintaining a manageable LTV. This capital is used to support his second acquisition.

By the third stage, Carlos owns three properties with a combined rental income of $5,800 per month. His portfolio value has increased significantly, and his equity position continues to grow. Each property contributes to his overall financial strength, allowing him to qualify for further refinancing and expansion.

Carlos continues this process over several years, carefully managing his leverage and maintaining sufficient reserves. By the fifth stage, he owns five properties with a combined value exceeding $2 million and rental income of over $10,000 per month. His asset base has grown, and his ability to access capital has increased accordingly. Throughout this process, Carlos uses leverage stacking to enhance his purchasing power. He combines asset-based refinancing with other financing options, allowing him to acquire properties more efficiently. He also diversifies his portfolio across different property types and locations, reducing risk and increasing stability.

Carlos regularly evaluates his portfolio, identifying opportunities to refinance, reposition, or expand. By maintaining a disciplined approach, he ensures that each step contributes to his overall strategy. His success is not the result of a single transaction, but of a structured and repeatable process.

This example demonstrates how scaling can be achieved through consistent application of asset-based refinancing principles. It shows how equity can be recycled, how leverage can be layered, and how a portfolio can grow over time through strategic decision-making. It also highlights the importance of discipline, planning, and adaptability.

When you apply these strategies, you begin to build momentum. Each acquisition, each refinance, and each decision contributes to a larger system that becomes more powerful with each iteration. This is the essence of scaling a portfolio using asset-based refinancing—a process that transforms individual opportunities into a comprehensive wealth-building engine.

Chapter 8

Exit Strategies, Portfolio Optimization, and Long-Term Wealth Preservation

As your portfolio grows through asset-based refinancing, a new phase of financial strategy emerges—one that is often overlooked in the pursuit of expansion. This phase is optimization and exit planning. While building and scaling are essential, long-term success ultimately depends on how well you manage, protect, and eventually transition your wealth. Asset-based refinancing is not just a tool for growth; it is also a powerful instrument for restructuring, stabilizing, and preparing your portfolio for the future. In this chapter, you will learn how to design exit strategies, optimize your holdings, and preserve wealth across changing market conditions and life stages.

The concept of an "exit" does not necessarily mean selling everything and stepping away. Instead, it refers to intentional decision-making about how and when to transition assets, reduce risk, or convert equity into different forms of value. For some, this may involve selling select properties to realize gains. For others, it may involve refinancing into more stable structures, reducing leverage, or repositioning assets to generate passive income. The key is that these decisions are made proactively, not reactively.

Portfolio optimization begins with evaluation. As your portfolio expands, not all assets will perform equally. Some properties may appreciate faster, generate higher cash flow, or present better refinancing opportunities. Others may underperform or require disproportionate effort to manage. Regularly reviewing your portfolio allows you to identify which assets are contributing most effectively to your goals. This process is not about eliminating assets arbitrarily—it is about aligning your holdings with your long-term strategy.

One of the most effective optimization strategies is strategic refinancing. Instead of using refinancing solely for expansion, you can use it to improve the structure of your existing portfolio. This may involve consolidating multiple loans into a single, more efficient structure, securing lower interest rates, or extending loan terms to improve cash flow. Asset-based refinancing provides the flexibility to make these adjustments without being constrained by traditional income requirements.

Deleveraging is another important consideration. While leverage is a powerful tool for growth, reducing leverage over time can enhance stability and preserve wealth. This does not mean eliminating debt entirely, but rather adjusting your leverage levels to reflect your evolving goals. For example, as you approach financial independence or retirement, you may choose to reduce LTV ratios, increase equity positions, and prioritize cash flow over expansion. Asset-based refinancing can facilitate this transition by allowing you to restructure your loans in a way that aligns with your new objectives.

Cash flow optimization becomes increasingly important in the later stages of portfolio development. While appreciation and equity growth drive early expansion, consistent income provides long-term stability. Refinancing into structures that lower monthly payments or increase net cash flow can enhance your financial position. This may involve extending loan terms, adjusting interest rates, or reallocating capital to higher-yield assets. The goal is to create a portfolio that not only grows, but also sustains itself.

Liquidity planning is also essential for long-term preservation. Even with a strong portfolio, a lack of accessible liquidity can create challenges. Asset-based refinancing allows you to maintain liquidity without selling assets, providing flexibility for both planned and unexpected needs. This liquidity can be used to cover expenses, fund new opportunities, or act as a buffer during market fluctuations. Maintaining a balance between invested capital and accessible funds is key to long-term resilience. Another dimension of exit strategy is tax efficiency. Selling assets can trigger capital gains taxes, which can significantly impact your net returns. By using refinancing as a tool for accessing equity, you may be able to defer or avoid these taxes while still benefiting from your wealth. Additionally, structuring your portfolio with tax considerations in mind can enhance overall efficiency. Working with tax professionals can help you navigate these complexities and optimize your strategy.

Legacy planning is an often-overlooked aspect of wealth preservation. As your portfolio grows, considering how it will be transferred or managed in the future becomes increasingly important. This may involve structuring ownership through entities, creating trusts, or planning for generational transfer. Asset-based refinancing can play a role in this process by providing liquidity and flexibility, allowing you to structure your assets in a way that aligns with your long-term vision.

Market cycles continue to influence your strategy even in the optimization phase. During strong markets, you may choose to realize gains or reposition assets. During downturns, maintaining liquidity and stability becomes more important. Understanding how to adapt your strategy to different market conditions ensures that your portfolio remains resilient over time. This adaptability is one of the key advantages of asset-based refinancing, as it allows you to adjust without being constrained by traditional lending limitations. Another important concept is selective liquidation. While the goal is often to preserve assets, there are times when selling certain properties can enhance your overall position. This may involve selling underperforming assets, consolidating holdings, or reallocating capital to more productive opportunities. The decision to sell should be based on strategy, not necessity. Asset-based refinancing can provide the liquidity needed to avoid forced sales, allowing you to make decisions from a position of strength.

Portfolio simplification is also worth considering. As portfolios grow, complexity can increase. Managing multiple properties, loans, and income streams can become challenging. Simplifying your portfolio—whether through consolidation, restructuring, or selective sales—can improve efficiency and reduce stress. The goal is to create a structure that is both effective and manageable.

The psychological aspect of transitioning from growth to preservation should not be underestimated. Many individuals become accustomed to expansion and find it difficult to shift focus toward stability. However, recognizing when to prioritize preservation is a key component of long-term success. This does not mean abandoning growth entirely, but rather balancing it with protection and sustainability. Ultimately, exit strategies and portfolio optimization are about control. They allow you to shape your financial future intentionally, rather than being influenced by external factors. Asset-based refinancing provides the flexibility to make these adjustments on your terms, ensuring that your portfolio remains aligned with your goals at every stage.

Real-Life Math Example: Optimizing and Transitioning a Mature Portfolio

Consider a borrower named Elena, a 62-year-old investor who has built a portfolio of six properties over the past decade using asset-based refinancing. Her portfolio includes a primary residence valued at $1,200,000 and five rental properties with a combined value of $2,800,000. Her total mortgage balance across all properties is $1,600,000, resulting in significant equity.

Elena also holds $900,000 in a brokerage account and $400,000 in retirement funds. Her goal is to transition from aggressive growth to stable income and long-term preservation while maintaining flexibility.

The first step in Elena's strategy is portfolio evaluation. She identifies that two of her rental properties are underperforming, generating lower returns relative to their value. She decides to sell one of these properties for $500,000, realizing a gain and reducing management complexity. After paying off the remaining loan balance of $250,000 on that property, she nets $250,000 before taxes.

Instead of reinvesting this capital immediately, Elena uses asset-based refinancing to restructure her remaining portfolio. She refinances her primary residence at a 60% LTV, resulting in a loan of $720,000. After paying off her existing balance of $400,000, she accesses $320,000 in cash. Combined with the proceeds from the property sale, she now has $570,000 in liquidity.

Elena uses a portion of this liquidity to pay down higher-interest loans on her remaining properties, reducing her overall debt and monthly obligations. She allocates $200,000 toward this purpose, significantly improving her cash flow. The remaining $370,000 is kept as a combination of reserves and low-risk investments.

Her new loan structure results in a total monthly mortgage obligation of approximately $9,000, while her rental income from the remaining properties is $11,500 per month. This creates a positive cash flow of $2,500 per month, providing stable income.

Elena also evaluates her asset base for qualification purposes. Her brokerage account and retirement funds are assessed, resulting in total eligible assets of approximately $1,180,000 after adjustments. Using a 120-month depletion model, her qualifying income is approximately $9,833 per month, supporting her refinanced structure.

Over the next several years, Elena's strategy focuses on preservation and stability. Her properties continue to appreciate, her cash flow remains consistent, and her reduced leverage provides protection against market fluctuations. She maintains strong reserves, ensuring that she can handle any unexpected changes.

By transitioning her strategy, Elena has shifted from rapid expansion to sustainable wealth management. She has optimized her portfolio, reduced risk, and created a reliable income stream. Importantly, she has done so without sacrificing flexibility, as her asset-based refinancing structure allows her to access additional liquidity if needed.

This example illustrates how asset-based refinancing can be used not only for growth, but also for optimization and preservation. It shows how strategic decisions—such as selective sales, refinancing, and debt reduction—can enhance long-term outcomes. It also highlights the importance of aligning your portfolio with your evolving goals.

When you apply these principles, you gain the ability to manage your wealth intentionally. You move from simply building a portfolio to shaping it in a way that supports your long-term vision. This is the essence of exit strategies and portfolio optimization—ensuring that the wealth you have built continues to serve you effectively for years to come.

Chapter 9

Creating Financial Freedom Through Asset-Based Refinancing

At its highest level, asset-based mortgage refinancing is not just a financial strategy—it is a pathway to financial freedom. Throughout this series, you have learned how to qualify using assets, extract equity, structure deals, manage risk, scale a portfolio, and optimize your holdings. Now, in this final chapter, everything comes together into a single outcome: the ability to design a life where your finances support your freedom, rather than limit it. Financial freedom is not defined by a specific number—it is defined by control, flexibility, and the ability to make decisions without being constrained by income requirements or financial pressure.

Financial freedom begins with understanding the relationship between assets, cash flow, and obligations. Traditional financial models emphasize income as the primary driver of lifestyle. In contrast, asset-based strategies shift the focus toward ownership and leverage. When your assets generate sufficient income or can be leveraged to provide liquidity, your dependence on earned income decreases. This transition is what allows you to move from working for money to having your money work for you. Asset-based refinancing accelerates this transition by unlocking the value of what you already own. Instead of waiting decades for equity to accumulate passively, you can actively access and deploy that equity to create additional income streams. This creates a compounding effect where each asset contributes to your overall financial position. Over time, the combined income and growth from your portfolio can replace or exceed traditional income sources, providing a foundation for financial independence.

One of the most important components of financial freedom is cash flow coverage. This occurs when your passive income is sufficient to cover your living expenses and financial obligations. Asset-based refinancing can help you achieve this by enabling you to acquire income-producing assets without liquidating your existing investments. By strategically deploying capital into properties or other opportunities that generate consistent income, you can build a portfolio that supports your lifestyle.

Another key element is flexibility. Financial freedom is not just about covering expenses—it is about having options. Asset-based refinancing provides access to liquidity that can be used for a wide range of purposes, from investing and business expansion to travel and personal goals. This flexibility allows you to adapt to changing circumstances and pursue opportunities without being restricted by cash flow limitations.

Debt, when used strategically, becomes a tool rather than a burden. In traditional thinking, debt is often viewed negatively. However, in the context of asset-based refinancing, debt is a mechanism for accessing capital and amplifying opportunity. The key is to ensure that your use of debt is aligned with your goals and supported by your assets and cash flow. When structured properly, debt can enhance your financial position rather than detract from it.

Time is another critical factor in achieving financial freedom. The earlier you begin implementing asset-based strategies, the more time your portfolio has to grow and compound. However, it is never too late to start. Whether you are in the early stages of building wealth or transitioning toward preservation, asset-based refinancing provides a framework that can be adapted to your situation. The key is consistency—applying the principles you have learned in a disciplined and intentional manner.

Another dimension of financial freedom is resilience. True freedom is not just about growth—it is about stability. Your financial system should be able to withstand market fluctuations, unexpected expenses, and changes in income.

This requires maintaining reserves, managing leverage, and diversifying your assets. Asset-based refinancing supports resilience by providing access to liquidity and flexibility, allowing you to navigate challenges without compromising your long-term strategy.

Lifestyle design is where financial freedom becomes tangible. As your portfolio grows and your cash flow increases, you gain the ability to shape your life according to your preferences. This may involve reducing work hours, pursuing passions, traveling, or spending more time with family. The goal is not simply to accumulate wealth, but to use that wealth to enhance your quality of life. Asset-based refinancing provides the tools to make this possible by aligning your financial resources with your personal goals.

Another important aspect is legacy. Financial freedom extends beyond your own lifetime. The systems you build, the assets you accumulate, and the strategies you implement can be passed on to future generations. By structuring your portfolio thoughtfully and maintaining flexibility through asset-based refinancing, you create a foundation that can support your family and provide opportunities for years to come.

The transition to financial freedom is not a single event—it is a process. It involves moving through stages of accumulation, expansion, optimization, and preservation. Each stage builds on the previous one, creating a progression that leads to greater control and independence. Asset-based refinancing is the thread that connects these stages, providing a consistent framework for accessing and deploying capital.

As you reach this point, it is important to recognize that financial freedom is both a destination and a mindset. It requires a shift in how you view money, assets, and opportunity. Instead of focusing solely on earning, you begin to focus on structuring and leveraging what you already have. This shift is what allows you to break free from traditional limitations and create a system that works for you.

Ultimately, the purpose of this chapter is to bring everything together into a clear and actionable vision. Financial freedom is not reserved for a select few—it is achievable through knowledge, strategy, and consistent execution. Asset-based refinancing provides the tools, but it is your decisions that determine the outcome. By applying the principles you have learned, you can create a financial system that supports your goals, enhances your lifestyle, and provides lasting security.

Real-Life Math Example: Achieving Financial Freedom Through Asset-Based Refinancing

Consider a borrower named Victor, a 53-year-old investor who begins with a primary residence valued at $1,000,000 and a mortgage balance of $300,000. Victor also has $800,000 in a brokerage account and $300,000 in retirement funds. His goal is to achieve financial freedom by building a portfolio that generates sufficient income to cover his living expenses of $8,000 per month.

In the first stage, Victor performs an asset-based cash-out refinance on his primary residence at a 70% LTV. The new loan amount is $700,000. After paying off his existing mortgage, he accesses $400,000 in cash. His assets are evaluated, with his brokerage account fully counted and his retirement account discounted to $210,000, resulting in total eligible assets of $1,010,000. Using a 120-month depletion model, his qualifying income is approximately $8,417 per month.

Victor uses $300,000 of his cash-out proceeds to acquire two rental properties, each generating $2,000 per month in income. He retains $100,000 as reserves. His total rental income is now $4,000 per month.

In the second stage, Victor refinances one of the rental properties after it appreciates in value. He accesses an additional $50,000 in equity, which he combines with savings to acquire a third property generating $1,800 per month. His total rental income increases to $5,800 per month.

Simultaneously, his investment portfolio continues to grow. Assuming a modest annual return of 6%, his $800,000 brokerage account generates approximately $48,000 per year, or $4,000 per month. Combined with his rental income, Victor now has $9,800 per month in total income.

At this point, Victor's income exceeds his living expenses of $8,000 per month. He has achieved cash flow coverage, a key milestone in financial freedom. Importantly, he has done so without liquidating his assets, allowing his portfolio to continue growing.

In the third stage, Victor focuses on optimization. He refinances his properties to improve terms and reduce his monthly obligations. He maintains strong reserves and diversifies his investments, ensuring stability. His portfolio continues to appreciate, further increasing his equity and financial flexibility.

Over time, Victor's system becomes self-sustaining. His assets generate income, his equity provides liquidity, and his financial structure supports his lifestyle. He no longer depends on earned income, giving him the freedom to make decisions based on preference rather than necessity.

This example demonstrates how asset-based refinancing can be used to achieve financial freedom. It shows how equity can be transformed into income-producing assets, how portfolios can be structured for growth and stability, and how consistent application of these principles can lead to independence. When you apply this approach, you move beyond traditional financial limitations and into a system designed for flexibility and control. You gain the ability to shape your financial future, create opportunities, and live on your own terms. This is the ultimate goal of asset-based refinancing—not just to build wealth, but to create freedom.

Chapter 10

Engineering the Ultimate Asset-Based Mortgage Strategy

At this final stage, you are no longer simply learning how asset-based mortgage refinancing works—you are now in a position to engineer it. Engineering is the highest level of financial strategy. It is where knowledge, experience, and intention come together to create a system that is customized, scalable, and resilient. This chapter is about bringing together every concept you have learned and designing a complete, adaptable framework that allows you to control your financial future with precision. This is not about following a formula—it is about creating your own.

Financial engineering begins with integration. Up to this point, you have explored individual components: qualification, liquidity, leverage, timing, scaling, optimization, and financial freedom. Now, the objective is to integrate these components into a cohesive system. Each part must work in harmony with the others. Your refinancing strategy must align with your investment goals. Your leverage must be supported by your cash flow. Your liquidity must be balanced with your long-term growth. When these elements are aligned, your financial system becomes both powerful and efficient.

The first step in engineering your strategy is defining your financial architecture. This involves mapping out your assets, liabilities, income streams, and goals. Think of this as the blueprint of your financial system. It includes your properties, investment accounts, reserves, and any other assets that contribute to your overall position. It also includes your debts, obligations, and risk exposure. By clearly understanding this architecture, you can identify where opportunities exist and how to structure your next move.

The second step is designing your capital flow. Capital flow refers to how money moves through your system. In an engineered strategy, capital is not static—it is constantly being repositioned. Equity is extracted, deployed into new opportunities, and then recycled as those opportunities grow. This flow creates momentum. The key is to ensure that each movement of capital is intentional and contributes to your overall objectives. This requires planning, discipline, and a clear understanding of your priorities.

Leverage calibration is another critical component. At this level, leverage is no longer viewed as a simple ratio—it is a dynamic variable that can be adjusted based on conditions and goals. You may choose to increase leverage during periods of growth and opportunity, and reduce it during periods of uncertainty or consolidation. This flexibility allows you to adapt your strategy without disrupting your system. The ability to calibrate leverage effectively is what separates advanced strategies from basic ones.

Another important element is scenario planning. Engineering your strategy means preparing for multiple outcomes, not just the ideal scenario. This involves modeling different possibilities, such as changes in interest rates, property values, or income streams. By understanding how your system performs under various conditions, you can identify potential weaknesses and strengthen them in advance. This proactive approach reduces risk and increases confidence in your decisions.

The concept of redundancy also plays a role. In engineering, redundancy refers to having backup systems in place. In financial terms, this means having multiple sources of liquidity, diversified assets, and alternative strategies. If one component of your system is affected, others can support it. This redundancy enhances resilience and ensures that your system can continue to function under a wide range of conditions.

Another advanced concept is optimization layering. This involves continuously refining your system to improve efficiency and performance. For example, you may refinance a property to lower your interest rate, restructure your loans to improve cash flow, or reallocate capital to higher-performing investments. These adjustments may seem incremental, but over time they can have a significant impact on your overall results. Optimization is an ongoing process, not a one-time event.

Control is a defining characteristic of an engineered strategy. Instead of reacting to external factors, you are actively shaping your financial environment. You decide when to refinance, how much equity to extract, where to deploy capital, and how to structure your obligations. This level of control allows you to operate with confidence and clarity, even in changing market conditions.

Another key element is scalability. Your strategy should be designed to grow with you. As your assets increase and your experience deepens, your system should be able to accommodate larger transactions, more complex structures, and greater opportunities. This requires building a foundation that is both strong and flexible. Asset-based refinancing supports scalability by providing access to capital without being constrained by traditional income limitations.

Long-term sustainability is what ensures that your strategy endures. Growth without sustainability can lead to instability, while sustainability without growth can limit potential. The goal is to achieve both. This involves maintaining balance, managing risk, and continuously aligning your actions with your objectives. An engineered strategy is one that can evolve over time while remaining grounded in sound principles.

Another dimension of engineering is personalization. No two financial systems are identical. Your strategy should reflect your goals, your risk tolerance, your resources, and your vision for the future. Asset-based refinancing provides the flexibility to customize your approach, allowing you to create a system that is uniquely suited to your situation.

The final component is execution. Even the most well-designed strategy requires action. Execution involves implementing your plan, monitoring your results, and making adjustments as needed. It requires discipline, attention to detail, and a commitment to continuous improvement. The ability to execute consistently is what turns strategy into results.

As you bring all of these elements together, you begin to see your financial system as a living structure—one that evolves, adapts, and grows over time. Asset-based refinancing is the engine that powers this structure, providing the liquidity and flexibility needed to move forward. By engineering your strategy, you move beyond individual transactions and into a comprehensive approach to wealth creation and management.

Real-Life Math Example: Engineering a Complete Asset-Based Strategy

Consider a borrower named Daniel, a 50-year-old investor with a primary residence valued at $1,100,000 and a mortgage balance of $300,000. Daniel also has $900,000 in a brokerage account, $400,000 in retirement funds, and $200,000 in cash. His goal is to engineer a system that generates consistent income, supports continued growth, and provides long-term stability.

The first step is establishing his financial architecture. Daniel's total assets include his home, investment accounts, and cash reserves. His liabilities include his existing mortgage. His goal is to increase his income to $10,000 per month while maintaining flexibility and growth potential.

Daniel begins by performing an asset-based cash-out refinance on his primary residence at a 70% LTV. The new loan amount is $770,000. After paying off his existing mortgage, he accesses $470,000 in cash. His assets are evaluated, with his brokerage account fully counted and his retirement account discounted to $280,000, resulting in total eligible assets of $1,180,000. Using a 120-month depletion model, his qualifying income is approximately $9,833 per month. Daniel allocates his capital strategically. He invests $350,000 into two rental properties, each generating $2,200 per month, for a total of $4,400 in rental income. He retains $120,000 as reserves. His new mortgage payment is approximately $4,900 per month, leaving a manageable gap that is partially offset by rental income.

In the second phase, Daniel focuses on capital flow. Over the next two years, his properties appreciate, and his rental income remains stable. He refinances one of the rental properties, accessing $60,000 in additional equity. Combined with savings, he uses this capital to acquire a third property generating $2,000 per month.

At this point, Daniel's total rental income is $6,400 per month. His investment portfolio continues to grow, generating approximately $4,500 per month in returns. Combined, his income exceeds his $10,000 target.

Daniel then calibrates his leverage. He refinances his primary residence at a slightly lower LTV, reducing his risk while maintaining access to liquidity. He also pays down a portion of his higher-interest debt, improving his cash flow.

Through scenario planning, Daniel evaluates potential changes in market conditions. He ensures that his reserves are sufficient to cover 18 months of expenses and that his portfolio remains diversified. This preparation enhances his confidence and stability. Over time, Daniel continues to optimize his system. He refinances properties to improve terms, reallocates capital to higher-performing investments, and maintains a balance between growth and preservation. His strategy evolves, but the core principles remain consistent.

This example illustrates how asset-based refinancing can be engineered into a comprehensive financial system. It shows how each component—architecture, capital flow, leverage, and optimization—works together to create a cohesive strategy. It also demonstrates the importance of adaptability, discipline, and continuous improvement.

When you reach this level, you are no longer simply participating in the financial system—you are designing it. You have the ability to shape your outcomes, control your resources, and create a structure that supports your goals. This is the essence of engineering the ultimate asset-based mortgage strategy—a process that transforms knowledge into mastery and strategy into lasting success.

Chapter 11

Mastering Consistency, Discipline, and Long-Term Execution

At the highest level of asset-based mortgage refinancing, success is no longer determined by knowledge alone—it is determined by consistency and execution. By now, you understand how to qualify using assets, extract equity, structure deals, scale a portfolio, optimize holdings, and engineer a complete financial system. However, none of these strategies produce meaningful results without disciplined application over time. This chapter focuses on the most overlooked yet most critical element of long-term success: the ability to execute consistently, refine continuously, and remain committed to your strategy regardless of short-term fluctuations.

Consistency is what transforms isolated wins into lasting wealth. Many individuals successfully complete one refinance, acquire one property, or execute one strong investment—but fail to repeat the process. Without repetition, the compounding effect is lost. Asset-based refinancing is most powerful when it becomes a habit, a system that is revisited and refined at regular intervals. Each cycle builds on the previous one, creating momentum that accelerates over time.

The goal is not perfection in any single transaction, but progress across many.

Discipline is what protects your system from breakdown. As your portfolio grows and your access to capital increases, so does the potential for overextension. The temptation to take on more leverage, pursue marginal opportunities, or deviate from your strategy can become stronger. Discipline ensures that your decisions remain aligned with your long-term objectives. This means adhering to your criteria for refinancing, maintaining appropriate leverage levels, and resisting the urge to act impulsively. Discipline is not about restriction—it is about maintaining control.

Long-term execution requires a shift in perspective. Instead of focusing on immediate results, you begin to think in terms of years and decades. Asset-based refinancing is not a quick path to wealth—it is a structured approach that compounds over time. This requires patience and the ability to stay committed even when progress feels gradual. Understanding that each step contributes to a larger system allows you to remain focused on the bigger picture.

Tracking and measurement are essential for maintaining consistency. A well-executed strategy is one that is monitored and evaluated regularly. This includes tracking your equity positions, cash flow, loan balances, asset growth, and overall net worth. By maintaining clear visibility into your financial system, you can identify trends, measure progress, and make informed adjustments. This level of awareness ensures that your strategy remains effective and aligned with your goals.

Another important aspect of execution is process standardization. As you repeat your refinancing and investment cycles, developing a consistent process can improve efficiency and reduce errors. This may include creating checklists for refinancing, standardizing documentation, or establishing criteria for evaluating opportunities. Standardization allows you to execute more quickly and confidently, particularly as your portfolio grows in complexity.

Adaptability is also critical. While consistency is important, it does not mean rigidity. Markets change, opportunities evolve, and your personal circumstances may shift. The ability to adapt your strategy while maintaining its core principles ensures that your system remains relevant and effective. This balance between consistency and adaptability is what allows long-term strategies to endure.

Another key element is resilience. Financial journeys are rarely linear. There will be periods of growth, as well as periods of challenge. Market downturns, unexpected expenses, or changes in conditions can test your strategy. Resilience allows you to navigate these challenges without abandoning your system. Maintaining reserves, managing risk, and staying committed to your long-term vision are all part of building resilience.

The concept of incremental improvement is also valuable. Each cycle of refinancing and investment provides an opportunity to learn and refine your approach. Small improvements in structuring, timing, or execution can have a significant impact over time. By continuously seeking to improve, you enhance the effectiveness of your system and increase your overall results.

Another important factor is focus. As your knowledge and resources expand, so do your options. While this can be beneficial, it can also lead to distraction. Staying focused on your core strategy ensures that your efforts remain concentrated and effective. This does not mean ignoring new opportunities, but rather evaluating them in the context of your overall system.

Accountability can further strengthen your execution. Whether through personal tracking, professional advisors, or partnerships, having mechanisms in place to hold yourself accountable can improve consistency. Accountability ensures that your plans are translated into action and that your strategy is implemented as intended.

Time management also plays a role in long-term execution. Building and managing a portfolio requires attention and effort. Allocating time to review your strategy, monitor your assets, and plan your next steps ensures that your system continues to function effectively. This does not require constant attention, but it does require intentional engagement.

Another dimension of execution is confidence. As you gain experience and see results, your confidence in the system grows. This confidence allows you to act decisively and avoid hesitation. However, it is important to balance confidence with caution, ensuring that your decisions remain grounded in analysis and strategy.

Ultimately, mastering consistency and discipline is what transforms asset-based refinancing from a strategy into a lifestyle. It becomes a natural part of how you manage your finances, make decisions, and pursue opportunities. This level of integration is what allows you to achieve and sustain long-term success.

Real-Life Math Example: The Power of Consistent Execution Over Time

Consider a borrower named Marcus, a 47-year-old investor who begins with a primary residence valued at $900,000 and a mortgage balance of $300,000. Marcus also has $600,000 in a brokerage account and $200,000 in retirement funds. His goal is to build long-term wealth through consistent application of asset-based refinancing. In the first year, Marcus performs a cash-out refinance at a 70% LTV, resulting in a new loan of $630,000. After paying off his existing mortgage, he accesses $330,000 in cash. His assets are evaluated, with his brokerage account fully counted and his retirement account discounted to $140,000, resulting in total eligible assets of $740,000. Using a 120-month depletion model, his qualifying income is approximately $6,167 per month.

Marcus uses $250,000 to acquire a rental property generating $2,100 per month and retains $80,000 as reserves. Over the next two years, he focuses on stability, allowing his property to appreciate and his portfolio to grow.

In year three, Marcus repeats the process. His primary residence has appreciated to $1,000,000, and his rental property is now valued at $320,000. He refinances his primary residence again, accessing an additional $100,000 in equity. Combined with savings, he acquires a second rental property generating $2,000 per month.

By year five, Marcus owns three properties with a combined rental income of $6,100 per month. His investment portfolio has grown to $750,000, generating approximately $3,750 per month in returns. His total income now approaches $9,850 per month. Marcus continues this process every two to three years, carefully managing his leverage and maintaining reserves. By year ten, he owns five properties with a combined value exceeding $2.5 million and rental income of over $10,000 per month. His investment portfolio has grown to over $1 million, generating additional income.

Throughout this period, Marcus remains consistent. He does not rush into decisions or deviate from his strategy. Each refinance is carefully planned, each investment is evaluated, and each step is aligned with his long-term goals. His success is not the result of extraordinary actions, but of disciplined repetition.

If Marcus had stopped after his first or second transaction, his results would have been limited. It is the consistency of his actions that creates exponential growth. Each cycle builds on the previous one, creating a compounding effect that accelerates over time.

This example demonstrates the power of long-term execution. It shows how small, consistent actions can lead to significant outcomes when applied over time. It also highlights the importance of discipline, patience, and focus in achieving financial success.

When you apply these principles, you move beyond short-term thinking and into a sustained approach to wealth building. You begin to see how each decision contributes to a larger system and how that system evolves over time. This is the essence of mastering consistency and discipline—turning strategy into results through deliberate and repeated action.

Chapter 12

The Legacy Blueprint—Turning Asset-Based Strategies Into Generational Wealth

At the highest level of financial mastery, the objective expands beyond personal success and into legacy. Asset-based mortgage refinancing, when fully understood and consistently applied, becomes more than a tool for liquidity or portfolio growth—it becomes a system capable of supporting multiple generations. This chapter is about designing that system intentionally. It is about creating a structure where your assets, strategies, and financial discipline extend beyond your lifetime, providing stability, opportunity, and education for those who follow.

Legacy begins with clarity of vision. Without a defined purpose, even the most successful financial systems can lose direction over time. You must decide what your wealth is meant to accomplish. Is it to provide financial security for your family, to fund education, to support entrepreneurial ventures, or to create a lasting financial foundation that continues to grow? This vision becomes the guiding force behind every decision you make. Asset-based refinancing allows you to structure your wealth in a way that aligns with this vision, ensuring that your resources are both accessible and sustainable.

One of the most important elements of a legacy blueprint is ownership structure. How your assets are held can significantly impact their long-term effectiveness. Holding properties and investments in the appropriate entities—such as trusts or business structures—can provide benefits related to control, protection, and transferability. Asset-based refinancing integrates well with these structures, as it allows you to maintain liquidity and flexibility while organizing your assets in a way that supports long-term goals.

Another key component is continuity. A legacy system must be able to function without constant intervention. This means creating processes, documentation, and frameworks that can be understood and followed by others. Your refinancing strategy, investment criteria, and risk management principles should be clearly defined and repeatable. This ensures that the system you have built does not depend solely on your direct involvement, but can continue to operate effectively over time.

Education plays a critical role in legacy building. Financial systems are only as strong as the people who manage them. Passing on knowledge, not just assets, is essential. This includes teaching the principles of asset-based refinancing, leverage, risk management, and strategic decision-making. When the next generation understands how the system works, they are better equipped to maintain and expand it. Without this understanding, even significant wealth can diminish over time.

Another important concept is intergenerational leverage. Asset-based refinancing allows future generations to access capital without needing to liquidate inherited assets. This means that the system you create can continue to generate opportunities long after it is established. For example, properties that have appreciated over time can be refinanced to fund new investments, creating a cycle of growth that spans generations. This continuity of opportunity is what transforms wealth into legacy.

Preservation is equally important as growth. While expansion drives wealth creation, preservation ensures that it endures. This involves managing risk, maintaining appropriate leverage levels, and ensuring that your portfolio remains resilient under different conditions. Asset-based refinancing supports preservation by providing liquidity without requiring asset sales, allowing you to protect your core holdings while still accessing capital when needed.

Another dimension of legacy planning is income sustainability. A strong legacy system generates consistent income that can support multiple beneficiaries. This may come from rental properties, investment returns, or other income-producing assets. By structuring your portfolio to prioritize stable cash flow, you create a foundation that can provide ongoing support. Asset-based refinancing can be used to optimize this income by improving loan terms, reducing costs, or reallocating capital to higher-performing assets.

Flexibility is also essential. Future conditions will differ from the present, and your system must be able to adapt. Asset-based refinancing provides this flexibility by allowing adjustments to be made as needed. Whether it involves accessing additional liquidity, restructuring loans, or repositioning assets, the ability to adapt ensures that your legacy remains relevant and effective.

Another key aspect is governance. Establishing clear guidelines for decision-making helps ensure that your system is managed consistently. This may include defining roles, responsibilities, and criteria for financial decisions. Governance provides structure and reduces the likelihood of mismanagement. It also creates a framework for accountability, ensuring that your strategy is implemented as intended.

The emotional and psychological aspects of legacy should not be overlooked. Wealth can create both opportunities and challenges for future generations. Instilling values such as discipline, responsibility, and long-term thinking is essential. These values support the effective management of the system and ensure that it continues to grow rather than diminish.

Asset-based refinancing also allows for strategic distribution. Instead of transferring assets outright, you can structure distributions in a way that maintains the integrity of the system. For example, providing access to income or liquidity while preserving core assets ensures that the foundation remains intact. This approach balances immediate benefits with long-term sustainability.

Another important concept is compounding across generations. When a system is maintained and expanded over time, the effects of compounding become exponential. Each generation builds upon the previous one, increasing the scale and impact of the portfolio. Asset-based refinancing supports this compounding by enabling continuous access to capital and opportunities.

Ultimately, the goal of this chapter is to help you see beyond individual transactions and even beyond your own lifetime. It is about creating a system that is designed to endure, evolve, and expand. Asset-based refinancing provides the tools, but it is your vision and execution that determine the outcome. By combining strategy, structure, and education, you can create a legacy that extends far into the future.

Real-Life Math Example: Building a Multi-Generational Asset-Based System

Consider a borrower named Robert, a 55-year-old investor who has built a portfolio consisting of a primary residence valued at $1,200,000 and four rental properties with a combined value of $2,000,000. His total mortgage balance across all properties is $1,200,000, and he holds $1,000,000 in a brokerage account and $400,000 in retirement funds.

Robert's goal is to create a system that generates consistent income for his family while preserving and expanding the portfolio over time. He begins by evaluating his assets and restructuring his loans using asset-based refinancing. By refinancing his primary residence at a 65% LTV, he secures a loan of $780,000. After paying off his existing balance of $400,000, he accesses $380,000 in liquidity.

Robert uses $250,000 of this capital to acquire an additional rental property generating $2,300 per month. He retains $130,000 as reserves. His total rental income across all properties now exceeds $9,500 per month.

His assets are evaluated for qualification purposes, with his brokerage account fully counted and his retirement funds discounted to $280,000. This results in total eligible assets of $1,280,000. Using a 120-month depletion model, his qualifying income is approximately $10,667 per month, supporting his refinanced structure.

Over the next five years, Robert's portfolio appreciates, and his rental income increases to over $12,000 per month. He introduces his children to the system, teaching them how the portfolio is structured and how asset-based refinancing is used to access and deploy capital.

As part of his legacy plan, Robert establishes a trust to hold his properties. This ensures that ownership can be transferred efficiently while maintaining control and structure. The trust also defines guidelines for how the portfolio should be managed, including criteria for refinancing, investment, and distribution.

When Robert transitions into retirement, his portfolio continues to generate income, supporting both his lifestyle and his family. His children, now familiar with the system, begin to participate in its management. They use asset-based refinancing to access equity and acquire additional properties, expanding the portfolio further.

By the second generation, the portfolio has grown to include eight properties with a combined value exceeding $5 million. Rental income provides financial stability, while refinancing continues to create opportunities for expansion. The system remains intact because it was designed with continuity, education, and structure in mind.

This example illustrates how asset-based refinancing can be used to create a legacy system that extends beyond a single lifetime. It shows how equity can be continuously recycled, how income can support multiple generations, and how knowledge and structure can preserve and expand wealth over time.

When you apply these principles, you move beyond personal success and into generational impact. You create a system that not only supports your goals, but also provides opportunities for those who follow. This is the ultimate expression of asset-based mortgage refinancing—a strategy that transforms wealth into legacy and potential into permanence.

Chapter 13

Building an Automated Asset-Based Wealth Machine

At this stage in your journey, you have learned how to think differently, structure strategically, and execute consistently. Now, the next evolution is automation—transforming your asset-based refinancing strategy into a system that operates with efficiency, predictability, and minimal friction. Automation does not mean removing control; it means enhancing it. It allows you to create a financial machine that continues to function, grow, and optimize even when you are not actively managing every detail. This chapter is about designing that machine and understanding how to make your wealth-building process scalable, efficient, and sustainable.

Automation begins with simplification. Before you can automate anything, you must clearly define the core components of your system. These include your refinancing criteria, your investment strategy, your risk management guidelines, and your cash flow targets. By reducing complexity into clear, repeatable steps, you create a foundation that can be systematized. This clarity is what allows you to move from manual decision-making to structured execution. One of the most important areas to automate is decision-making criteria.

Instead of evaluating each opportunity from scratch, you establish predefined rules. For example, you may decide that you will refinance when your property reaches a certain loan-to-value threshold, or that you will invest in properties that meet specific cash flow and appreciation criteria. These rules remove uncertainty and ensure that your decisions remain consistent over time. They also reduce the influence of emotion, allowing your strategy to operate based on logic and structure.

Data tracking is another critical component of automation. Your financial system generates a constant flow of information—property values, loan balances, rental income, asset performance, and more. By organizing and tracking this data systematically, you create visibility into your system's performance. This allows you to identify opportunities, monitor progress, and make informed adjustments. Technology plays a key role here, enabling you to track and analyze your financial metrics efficiently.

Process automation further enhances efficiency. This includes streamlining tasks such as document preparation, loan applications, property analysis, and financial reporting. By creating templates, checklists, and workflows, you reduce the time and effort required to execute each step. This not only improves efficiency but also reduces the likelihood of errors.

As your portfolio grows, these efficiencies become increasingly valuable.

Another important aspect of automation is delegation. You do not need to manage every detail yourself. By working with professionals—such as lenders, property managers, accountants, and advisors—you can distribute responsibilities across a team. This allows you to focus on strategy while ensuring that operational tasks are handled effectively. Delegation is not about relinquishing control; it is about optimizing how your time and resources are used.

Cash flow management can also be automated to a significant extent. Setting up systems for collecting rental income, paying expenses, and allocating funds ensures that your financial flows remain consistent. This reduces the need for constant oversight and allows your system to operate smoothly. Automation in this area also enhances discipline, ensuring that your financial priorities are consistently maintained.

Another key element is refinancing triggers. Instead of manually evaluating when to refinance, you can establish triggers based on specific conditions. For example, a certain level of property appreciation, a reduction in interest rates, or an increase in equity can signal the right time to act. By defining these triggers in advance, you create a system that identifies opportunities automatically, allowing you to act quickly and efficiently.

Scaling through automation requires a shift in focus from individual transactions to system performance. Instead of asking, "Is this a good deal?" you begin to ask, "Does this fit within my system?" This perspective ensures that each decision contributes to your overall strategy. It also allows you to manage a larger portfolio without becoming overwhelmed by complexity.

Risk management can also be integrated into your automated system. By setting limits on leverage, maintaining reserve requirements, and diversifying your assets, you create safeguards that operate consistently. These safeguards ensure that your system remains stable even as it grows. Automation in risk management provides a layer of protection that supports long-term sustainability.

Another advanced concept is feedback loops. Your system should not only operate automatically, but also learn and improve over time. By regularly reviewing performance metrics and outcomes, you can identify areas for improvement and adjust your processes accordingly. This continuous refinement enhances the effectiveness of your system and ensures that it evolves with changing conditions. Time efficiency is one of the most significant benefits of automation. By reducing the time required for routine tasks, you free up resources to focus on higher-level strategy and decision-making. This allows you to scale your efforts without proportionally increasing your workload. In essence, automation allows your system to do more with less.

Psychological benefits also play a role. A well-automated system reduces stress and uncertainty by providing structure and predictability. You no longer need to constantly monitor every detail or make decisions under pressure. Instead, you operate within a framework that guides your actions and supports your goals. This clarity enhances confidence and allows you to focus on long-term growth.

Another important aspect is adaptability. While automation provides structure, your system must remain flexible enough to adjust to new conditions. This means periodically reviewing and updating your criteria, processes, and strategies. Automation is not static—it is dynamic. It evolves as your knowledge, experience, and circumstances change.

Ultimately, building an automated asset-based wealth machine is about creating a system that works for you. It is about combining strategy, structure, and technology to create a process that is efficient, scalable, and sustainable.

Asset-based refinancing serves as the engine of this system, providing the liquidity and flexibility needed to keep it moving forward.

Real-Life Math Example: Automating a Scalable Asset-Based System

Consider a borrower named Steven, a 45-year-old investor who has built a portfolio consisting of a primary residence valued at $950,000 and two rental properties with a combined value of $600,000. His total mortgage balance across all properties is $500,000, and he holds $700,000 in a brokerage account and $200,000 in retirement funds.

Steven's goal is to create an automated system that allows him to scale his portfolio efficiently while minimizing manual effort. He begins by defining his criteria. He decides that he will refinance any property that reaches 70% LTV and will invest in properties that generate at least $2,000 per month in rental income.

In the first stage, Steven performs a cash-out refinance on his primary residence. At a value of $950,000, the maximum loan at 70% LTV is $665,000. After paying off his existing balance of $300,000, he accesses $365,000 in cash. His assets are evaluated, with his brokerage account fully counted and his retirement funds discounted to $140,000, resulting in total eligible assets of $840,000. Using a 120-month depletion model, his qualifying income is $7,000 per month. Steven uses $300,000 to acquire a new rental property generating $2,200 per month and retains $65,000 as reserves. He sets up automated systems for rent collection, expense payments, and financial tracking. This ensures that his cash flow is managed consistently without constant oversight.

Over the next two years, his properties appreciate, and his rental income increases. His system tracks property values and identifies that one of his rental properties has reached the 70% LTV threshold. This triggers a refinance, allowing Steven to access an additional $60,000 in equity. Combined with savings, he uses this capital to acquire another property.

By year five, Steven owns five properties with a combined value exceeding $2 million and rental income of over $9,000 per month. His system continues to operate efficiently, with automated tracking, predefined criteria, and delegated responsibilities. He spends less time managing day-to-day operations and more time focusing on strategy.

Steven also implements feedback loops, reviewing his system annually to identify improvements. He adjusts his criteria, refines his processes, and optimizes his portfolio. This continuous improvement ensures that his system remains effective and aligned with his goals. If Steven had relied on manual processes, managing this level of complexity would have been significantly more challenging. By automating his system, he is able to scale efficiently while maintaining control and consistency. His strategy becomes a machine—one that continues to generate opportunities and growth with minimal friction.

This example demonstrates how automation can enhance the effectiveness of asset-based refinancing. It shows how predefined criteria, data tracking, and streamlined processes can create a scalable system. It also highlights the importance of balancing automation with adaptability, ensuring that the system remains flexible and responsive.

When you apply these principles, you move beyond managing your finances and into designing a system that works for you. You create a structure that is efficient, scalable, and aligned with your goals. This is the essence of building an automated asset-based wealth machine—a system that transforms strategy into consistent, long-term results.

Chapter 14

The Infinite Wealth Loop—Sustaining Momentum for Life

At this level, your journey evolves from building, scaling, optimizing, and automating into something even more powerful: sustaining. The final stage of mastery in asset-based mortgage refinancing is creating what can be called the Infinite Wealth Loop—a self-reinforcing cycle where your assets continuously generate equity, your equity generates liquidity, your liquidity creates new assets, and your system repeats this process indefinitely. This is not a temporary phase. It is a lifelong framework that allows you to maintain momentum, adapt to change, and continuously expand your financial position without starting over.

The Infinite Wealth Loop begins with a simple but profound realization: wealth is not built in isolated transactions—it is built in cycles. Each refinance, each acquisition, each optimization step feeds into the next. When these cycles are aligned and executed consistently, they create a system that compounds not just financially, but structurally. Over time, your system becomes more efficient, more resilient, and more powerful. The first component of this loop is equity generation. Every property you own contributes to your equity through appreciation and principal reduction. This equity is the fuel of your system. Without it, there is nothing to extract, deploy, or recycle. Understanding how to grow equity—through strategic acquisitions, market selection, and property improvements—is essential. The stronger your equity base, the more powerful your loop becomes.

The second component is equity extraction. Asset-based refinancing allows you to access this equity without selling your assets. This is where the loop gains momentum. Instead of waiting for wealth to accumulate passively, you actively convert it into usable capital. The key is to extract equity strategically, ensuring that your leverage remains aligned with your overall risk tolerance and objectives.

The third component is capital deployment. Extracted equity must be used effectively to sustain the loop. This typically involves investing in income-producing assets that contribute to both cash flow and future equity growth. The quality of your deployment decisions directly impacts the strength of your system. Each investment should be evaluated not only on its individual merits, but on how it contributes to the overall loop.

The fourth component is income reinforcement. As your portfolio grows, the income generated by your assets becomes an increasingly important part of the system. This income supports your obligations, funds additional investments, and provides stability. Over time, it can also replace earned income, allowing you to operate with greater flexibility and independence.

The fifth component is system optimization. No system remains static. As your portfolio evolves, you must continuously refine your structure to maintain efficiency. This includes refinancing to improve terms, reallocating capital to higher-performing assets, and adjusting your leverage as needed. Optimization ensures that your loop remains effective and aligned with your goals.

Momentum is what transforms this cycle into an infinite loop. Each iteration builds on the previous one, increasing your capacity to generate equity, access capital, and create new opportunities. This momentum is not accidental—it is the result of consistent execution and strategic alignment. The more disciplined your approach, the stronger your momentum becomes.

Another critical aspect of sustaining the loop is maintaining balance. Growth and stability must coexist. While it is tempting to maximize every opportunity, overextension can disrupt the system. Maintaining appropriate leverage, sufficient reserves, and diversified assets ensures that your loop remains stable even as it expands. Balance is what allows the loop to continue indefinitely rather than collapse under its own weight.

Time plays a unique role in this stage. Unlike earlier phases, where time is used to build and scale, here it becomes a multiplier. Each year that your system operates effectively increases its strength. Compounding accelerates, opportunities expand, and your system becomes more self-sustaining. This is where patience and consistency deliver their greatest rewards.

Another important element is adaptability. Markets will change, opportunities will shift, and your personal goals may evolve. The Infinite Wealth Loop is not rigid—it is designed to adapt. Asset-based refinancing provides the flexibility needed to adjust your system without disrupting its core structure. This adaptability ensures that your loop remains relevant and effective over time.

The psychological shift at this stage is significant. You move from thinking about individual deals to thinking about system performance. Your focus shifts from short-term gains to long-term sustainability. This perspective allows you to make decisions that support the overall health of your system rather than reacting to isolated opportunities.

Another dimension of the loop is optionality. As your system grows, your options expand. You can choose to accelerate growth, focus on preservation, explore new opportunities, or simply maintain your current position. This flexibility is one of the greatest benefits of a well-designed system. It allows you to align your financial strategy with your lifestyle and goals at any given time.

Legacy integration also becomes more natural within the Infinite Wealth Loop. Because the system is designed to sustain itself, it can be passed on and continued by future generations. The same cycles of equity generation, extraction, and deployment can be repeated, creating a multi-generational framework for growth. This continuity is what transforms wealth into a lasting legacy.

Risk awareness remains essential. Even in a well-functioning system, risks must be monitored and managed. Market fluctuations, changes in lending conditions, and unexpected events can impact your system. By maintaining discipline, reserves, and diversification, you ensure that your loop can withstand these challenges.

Ultimately, the Infinite Wealth Loop represents the culmination of everything you have learned. It is a system that integrates knowledge, strategy, and execution into a continuous process of growth and sustainability. It is not dependent on a single opportunity or moment—it is designed to operate over a lifetime.

Real-Life Math Example: Sustaining the Infinite Wealth Loop

Consider a borrower named Adrian, a 52-year-old investor who has built a portfolio consisting of a primary residence valued at $1,200,000 and four rental properties with a combined value of $2,400,000. His total mortgage balance across all properties is $1,500,000, and he holds $800,000 in a brokerage account and $300,000 in retirement funds.

Adrian's goal is to sustain a system that continuously generates income, equity, and opportunities without requiring constant manual effort. He begins by evaluating his current equity position. His total property value is $3,600,000, and his total debt is $1,500,000, giving him $2,100,000 in equity.

In the first cycle, Adrian identifies that his primary residence has appreciated significantly. He performs an asset-based refinance at a 65% LTV, resulting in a loan of $780,000. After paying off his existing balance of $400,000, he accesses $380,000 in equity. His assets are evaluated, with his brokerage account fully counted and his retirement funds discounted to $210,000, resulting in total eligible assets of $1,010,000. Using a 120-month depletion model, his qualifying income is approximately $8,417 per month. Adrian deploys $300,000 of this capital into a new rental property generating $2,400 per month and retains $80,000 as reserves. His total rental income across all properties now exceeds $11,000 per month.

Over the next three years, his portfolio appreciates further. His new property increases in value to $400,000, and his existing properties continue to generate income and equity. Adrian's system tracks these changes and identifies opportunities for additional refinancing.

In the second cycle, Adrian refinances one of his rental properties, accessing $70,000 in additional equity. Combined with accumulated cash flow, he uses this capital to invest in another property. His portfolio now includes six properties with a combined value exceeding $4 million.

At this stage, Adrian's rental income exceeds $14,000 per month, covering his mortgage obligations and providing surplus income. His investment portfolio continues to grow, adding another layer of financial strength.

Adrian continues to repeat this process, carefully managing his leverage and maintaining sufficient reserves. Each cycle reinforces the previous one, creating a system that operates with increasing efficiency. His equity grows, his income expands, and his ability to access capital improves. Over a ten-year period, Adrian's portfolio grows to include eight properties with a combined value exceeding $6 million. His rental income provides significant financial flexibility, and his asset base continues to expand. Importantly, his system requires less active management as automation and structure take over.

This example illustrates how the Infinite Wealth Loop operates in practice. It shows how equity can be continuously generated, extracted, and deployed to create a self-sustaining system. It also highlights the importance of balance, discipline, and strategic decision-making in maintaining the loop.

When you apply these principles, you move beyond building wealth and into sustaining it. You create a system that works for you, adapts to change, and continues to grow over time. This is the ultimate expression of asset-based mortgage refinancing—a lifelong framework for financial momentum, stability, and opportunity.

Chapter 15

Living the System—Integrating Wealth, Lifestyle, and Purpose

At the final stage of mastery, your financial system is no longer something separate from your life—it becomes part of how you live. Asset-based mortgage refinancing, when fully integrated, is not just a strategy you use occasionally. It becomes a natural extension of your decision-making, your opportunities, and your lifestyle. This chapter is about that integration. It is about living within the system you have built, aligning your wealth with your daily life, and using your financial structure to support not only growth, but fulfillment and purpose.

The journey you have completed has taken you from understanding to execution, from execution to scaling, and from scaling to sustainability. Now, the focus shifts to alignment. Wealth without alignment can feel disconnected. It can create complexity without clarity, or opportunity without direction. True mastery comes when your financial system supports your personal goals, your values, and the way you want to live. Asset-based refinancing provides the flexibility to make this alignment possible. One of the most important aspects of living the system is intentional lifestyle design. Instead of structuring your life around income, you begin to structure your income around your life. Your portfolio, your cash flow, and your access to liquidity become tools that allow you to choose how you spend your time. Whether that means working less, pursuing new ventures, traveling, or focusing on personal growth, your system supports those choices. This is where financial strategy becomes deeply personal.

Time becomes one of your most valuable resources. As your system generates income and provides liquidity, your dependence on active work decreases. This creates the opportunity to reclaim your time and use it in ways that are meaningful to you. Asset-based refinancing plays a role here by allowing you to access capital without disrupting your investments, giving you the flexibility to make decisions based on preference rather than necessity.

Another key element is simplicity within complexity. While your financial system may be sophisticated, your day-to-day experience should not feel overwhelming. Through automation, delegation, and structured processes, you can manage a complex portfolio with relative ease. This allows you to focus on high-level decisions and personal priorities rather than being consumed by operational details.

Freedom of choice is one of the most powerful outcomes of this integration. When your system is functioning effectively, you are no longer limited by financial constraints. You can choose which opportunities to pursue, which risks to take, and which paths to follow. This freedom is not about avoiding responsibility—it is about having the ability to make decisions from a position of strength.

Another important dimension is purpose. Wealth, when aligned with purpose, becomes more than accumulation—it becomes a means of impact. This may involve supporting causes you care about, investing in projects that align with your values, or creating opportunities for others. Asset-based refinancing provides the resources and flexibility to pursue these objectives without compromising your financial foundation.

Balance remains essential even at this stage. While your system provides significant opportunities, maintaining a balance between growth, preservation, and lifestyle ensures long-term sustainability. This includes continuing to manage risk, maintaining reserves, and making thoughtful decisions about leverage. Balance allows you to enjoy the benefits of your system without undermining its stability.

Another key concept is presence. As your financial system becomes more automated and efficient, you gain the ability to be more present in your life. Instead of being constantly focused on financial concerns, you can direct your attention toward relationships, experiences, and personal development. This shift is one of the most meaningful outcomes of financial freedom.

Adaptability continues to play a role. Your goals, interests, and circumstances may evolve over time, and your system should evolve with them. Asset-based refinancing provides the flexibility to adjust your strategy as needed, ensuring that your financial structure remains aligned with your life. This adaptability allows you to navigate change with confidence and clarity.

Another important aspect is confidence. Living within a well-designed system provides a sense of stability and assurance. You understand how your finances work, how your assets are structured, and how your system responds to different conditions. This confidence allows you to make decisions decisively and pursue opportunities without hesitation.

Community and relationships also become more significant. As your financial system supports your lifestyle, you have the ability to invest more time and energy into meaningful connections. This may include family, friends, or professional networks. These relationships can enrich your life and create additional opportunities for growth and collaboration. Another dimension is continuous growth. Even at this stage, learning and improvement remain important. Markets evolve, strategies advance, and new opportunities emerge. Staying engaged and informed ensures that your system remains effective and aligned with current conditions. Growth is not just financial—it is intellectual and personal.

Legacy naturally integrates into this stage as well. The system you live within can be shared, taught, and passed on. By demonstrating how it works and involving others in its management, you create continuity. This ensures that the benefits of your system extend beyond your own experience and into future generations.

Ultimately, living the system is about harmony. It is about creating a financial structure that supports your life rather than complicates it. It is about using your resources intentionally, aligning your actions with your goals, and creating a life that reflects your values. Asset-based refinancing is the tool that makes this possible, but it is your vision and execution that bring it to life.

Real-Life Math Example: Living Within a Fully Integrated System

Consider a borrower named Sophia, a 55-year-old investor who has built a portfolio consisting of a primary residence valued at $1,300,000 and five rental properties with a combined value of $3,000,000. Her total mortgage balance across all properties is $1,800,000, and she holds $900,000 in a brokerage account and $300,000 in retirement funds.

Sophia's goal is no longer focused on rapid growth. Instead, she wants to live within her system, using it to support her lifestyle, provide stability, and create opportunities aligned with her interests.

Her portfolio generates $13,000 per month in rental income, while her investment portfolio produces approximately $4,500 per month in returns. Her total monthly income is $17,500, comfortably exceeding her living expenses of $10,000 per month.

Sophia evaluates her financial structure and decides to perform a strategic refinance on her primary residence. At a 60% LTV, she secures a loan of $780,000. After paying off her existing balance of $500,000, she accesses $280,000 in liquidity. Her assets are evaluated, resulting in total eligible assets of approximately $1,110,000 after adjustments. Using a

120-month depletion model, her qualifying income is approximately $9,250 per month.

Instead of deploying this capital into new acquisitions, Sophia uses it to enhance her lifestyle and flexibility. She allocates $100,000 toward travel and personal projects, $80,000 as additional reserves, and $100,000 into low-risk investments that provide steady returns.

Her monthly obligations remain manageable, with mortgage payments totaling approximately $9,500 per month. Her income continues to exceed her expenses, providing both stability and flexibility.

Sophia's system is largely automated. Rental income is collected automatically, expenses are managed through structured processes, and her portfolio is monitored using financial tracking tools. She spends minimal time on operational tasks and focuses primarily on strategic decisions and personal priorities.

Over time, her properties continue to appreciate, and her income remains consistent. She periodically refinances to optimize her structure, but these decisions are made with a focus on maintaining balance rather than maximizing growth.

Sophia also involves her family in her system, teaching them how it works and preparing them to manage it in the future. This integration ensures continuity and aligns her financial strategy with her legacy goals.

This example illustrates what it means to live within a financial system. It shows how asset-based refinancing can be used not only for growth, but for lifestyle, flexibility, and purpose. It demonstrates how a well-designed system can support both financial and personal objectives.

When you reach this stage, your financial strategy becomes a natural part of your life. It supports your choices, enhances your experiences, and provides a foundation for long-term fulfillment. This is the ultimate outcome of asset-based mortgage refinancing—not just building wealth, but living a life that reflects your goals, values, and vision.

Final Thoughts

The Power of Asset-Based Thinking and the Path Forward

As you reach the end of this journey through asset-based mortgage refinancing and equity access, it is important to pause and reflect on what you have truly gained. This is not just knowledge about a financial product or a lending strategy. What you now possess is a completely different way of thinking about money, assets, and opportunity. You have moved beyond the traditional limitations of income-based systems and into a framework where ownership, structure, and strategy define what is possible. This shift alone has the potential to change everything.

For most people, financial life is reactive. Income is earned, expenses are paid, and whatever remains is saved or invested. Opportunities are often missed because liquidity is limited, and decisions are constrained by monthly cash flow. Asset-based thinking breaks this cycle. It introduces a proactive approach where your existing resources—your properties, your investments, your accumulated equity—become tools that can be actively leveraged. Instead of waiting, you act. Instead of being constrained, you create options.

Throughout this series, you have seen how equity can be transformed from a static number into a dynamic force. You have learned how to extract it, deploy it, recycle it, and optimize it. You have seen how a single refinance can become the foundation for a broader system, and how that system can grow over time into something far greater than the sum of its parts. This is the essence of financial leverage—not just in the technical sense, but in the strategic sense. It is the ability to do more with what you already have.

But with this power comes responsibility. Asset-based refinancing is not a shortcut or a guarantee of success. It is a tool, and like any tool, its effectiveness depends on how it is used. The principles you have learned—discipline, risk management, strategic deployment, and long-term thinking—are what ensure that this tool works in your favor. Without them, even the best strategies can become unstable. With them, you create a system that is both powerful and sustainable.

One of the most important takeaways from this journey is the concept of intentionality. Every decision you make—whether it is refinancing a property, acquiring a new asset, or adjusting your leverage—should be guided by a clear purpose. This purpose connects your actions to your goals, ensuring that each step contributes to a larger vision. Without intentionality, it is easy to become reactive, chasing opportunities without fully understanding their impact. With intentionality, you move forward with clarity and confidence.

Another critical insight is the role of time. Asset-based strategies are most effective when applied consistently over time. The true power of this approach lies in compounding—not just in financial returns, but in knowledge, experience, and momentum. Each cycle of refinancing and reinvestment builds on the previous one, creating a progression that accelerates as it grows. This is why patience and persistence are so important. The results may not always be immediate, but they are cumulative and lasting.

You have also learned that flexibility is one of your greatest assets. Markets change, opportunities evolve, and circumstances shift. The ability to adapt your strategy without losing its core principles is what allows you to navigate these changes effectively. Asset-based refinancing provides this flexibility by giving you access to liquidity and control over your structure. It allows you to respond to new opportunities and challenges without being forced into reactive decisions.

The concept of control cannot be overstated. Traditional financial systems often place control in the hands of external factors—employers, lenders, or market conditions.

Asset-based strategies shift that control back to you. You decide when to access your equity, how to deploy your capital, and how to structure your obligations. This level of control is what enables you to shape your financial future rather than simply respond to it.

Another key theme is balance. Growth and preservation, leverage and stability, action and patience—these are not opposing forces, but complementary ones. The most successful strategies are those that balance these elements effectively. Too much focus on growth can lead to overextension, while too much focus on preservation can limit opportunity. Finding the right balance ensures that your system remains both dynamic and resilient.

As you move forward, it is important to remember that this journey is not about perfection. There will be decisions that work better than others, opportunities that are missed, and challenges that arise. What matters is not avoiding mistakes entirely, but learning from them and continuing to refine your approach. Each experience adds to your understanding, making your system stronger over time.

The idea of building a system is central to everything you have learned. Individual transactions are important, but they are not the end goal. The goal is to create a framework that can be repeated, scaled, and adapted. This framework becomes the foundation of your financial life, guiding your decisions and supporting your growth. Asset-based refinancing is the engine of this system, but it is your strategy that determines how it operates.

You have also seen how this approach extends beyond personal success into broader impact. Whether it is creating opportunities for your family, supporting future generations, or contributing to your community, the system you build can have far-reaching effects. This is where financial strategy becomes something more than numbers—it becomes a means of creating lasting value.

Another important realization is that financial freedom is not a single destination. It is a continuum. At different stages of your journey, your definition of freedom may evolve. Early on, it may be about creating additional income or reducing dependence on a job. Later, it may be about stability, flexibility, or legacy. Asset-based refinancing supports each of these stages by providing the tools needed to adapt and grow.

The mindset you carry forward is just as important as the strategies you implement. Asset-based thinking encourages you to see opportunities where others see limitations. It challenges you to think creatively, act strategically, and remain disciplined. This mindset is what allows you to unlock the full potential of the system you have built.

As you continue your journey, take the time to revisit the principles outlined in this series. Each chapter represents a layer of understanding that can be applied in different ways depending on your situation. By integrating these principles into your daily decision-making, you ensure that your strategy remains active and effective.

It is also important to surround yourself with the right resources and support. Whether it is working with experienced professionals, leveraging technology, or continuing your education, having the right tools and guidance can enhance your ability to execute. Success in asset-based refinancing is not achieved in isolation—it is supported by knowledge, relationships, and continuous learning.

Ultimately, the path forward is yours to define. The tools are in your hands, the knowledge is in your mind, and the opportunities are in front of you. What you do with them will determine the outcome. By approaching this journey with intention, discipline, and a commitment to growth, you can create a financial system that supports your goals and enhances your life.

The power of asset-based refinancing lies not just in what it allows you to do today, but in what it enables you to build over time. It is a strategy that evolves with you, adapts to your needs, and supports your vision. When used thoughtfully, it becomes more than a financial tool—it becomes a foundation for long-term success.

As you close this chapter, remember that this is not the end of your journey. It is the beginning of a new phase—one where you apply what you have learned, refine your approach, and continue to grow. The principles you have gained are not static; they are meant to be used, tested, and expanded upon. With each step, you move closer to a system that is uniquely yours.

And in that system, you will find something greater than wealth—you will find control, flexibility, and the ability to create a life on your own terms.

How to Get a Personalized Asset-Based Mortgage Review

If you found this book helpful, you may want to see how these concepts apply to your specific financial situation. Asset-based lending is highly customized—your assets, liquidity, credit profile, property type, and long-term goals all play a role in determining what you qualify for and how your loan should be structured.

Every borrower's situation is different. The type of assets you hold, how those assets are allocated, your credit history, the property you are purchasing or refinancing, and current lender guidelines all affect your options. The strategies and examples in this book are designed to teach you how asset-based mortgage loans work—but your actual qualifying income, loan amount, and structure can only be determined by reviewing your real numbers.

If you would like a no-obligation Asset-Based Mortgage review, you can request one here:

Email: **info@FinibiMortgage.com**

A licensed mortgage broker will review your assets, credit profile, and goals, and explain what asset-based mortgage options may be available to you—including asset depletion loans, investment property financing, refinancing strategies, and advanced structuring approaches tailored to your situation.

No cost. No pressure. No obligation.

Sincerely,

Joseph G. Correa

Finibi Mortgage Inc.

Licensed Mortgage Broker

About the Author

Joseph G. Correa is a licensed mortgage broker and the founder of Finibi Mortgage, a Florida-based brokerage specializing in asset-based mortgage lending, alternative financing, and strategic real estate funding solutions for homeowners, investors, and high-net-worth borrowers. With more than two decades of experience in mortgage lending, underwriting, and financial structuring, Joseph has helped thousands of clients qualify for real estate using assets instead of traditional income, unlocking opportunities that conventional lending often restricts.

Unlike traditional loan officers who focus solely on income-based approvals, Joseph's approach is centered on asset positioning, financial strategy, and long-term wealth building. He believes that mortgages should not be limited by outdated income rules, but instead structured around true financial strength—assets, liquidity, and intelligent leverage. This philosophy has made him a trusted advisor for entrepreneurs, retirees, self-employed individuals, and investors who need flexible financing solutions that align with how they actually build and manage wealth.

Joseph is widely recognized for his expertise in asset depletion mortgage loans, bank statement programs, non-QM lending, investment property financing, and advanced structuring strategies that allow borrowers to qualify without relying on tax returns or W-2 income. His ability to simplify complex underwriting guidelines into clear, actionable strategies has helped clients use their savings, investment portfolios, and retirement accounts to acquire real estate, scale portfolios, and preserve liquidity.

Through his education platform, Finibi Academy, Joseph has trained tens of thousands of students worldwide in mortgage strategy, credit optimization, real estate investing, and financial independence. His courses and books are designed for both beginners and experienced professionals who want a deeper understanding of how modern lending truly works beyond traditional income-based limitations.

Joseph created The Asset-Based Mortgage Mastery Series to provide a clear, practical roadmap for borrowers and professionals who want to leverage assets instead of income to qualify for real estate. His mission is simple: to help people understand how to use their assets as a powerful financial tool, eliminate unnecessary barriers to financing, and build long-term wealth through strategic lending.

When he is not structuring loans or writing, Joseph works with clients across the United States to design customized asset-based mortgage strategies that align with their financial goals, liquidity needs, and long-term investment plans.

The Asset-Based Mortgage Mastery Series Roadmap

The Professional Guide to Qualifying for Real Estate Using Assets, Not Income

The purpose of *The Asset-Based Mortgage Mastery Series* is to give borrowers, investors, and financial professionals the same strategies used by banks, private lenders, and institutional investors—translated into clear, practical guidance that can be applied in real life. This series is designed to take you from foundational understanding to advanced mastery of how to qualify for, structure, and scale real estate financing using assets instead of traditional income.

Each book builds on the last. You are not just learning how to get approved—you are learning how to think, structure, and operate like the institutions that control capital.

Book 1 — Asset-Based Mortgage Loan Fundamentals

This book gives you the foundation. You will understand how asset-based mortgage loans work, how asset depletion is calculated, how lenders evaluate risk, and why income is no longer the only path to qualification. This is where you shift your mindset from income-based borrowing to asset-based strategy.

Book 2 — Retirement Asset Mortgage Qualification

This book focuses on using retirement accounts such as

401(k)s, IRAs, and investment portfolios to qualify for mortgage loans. You will learn how lenders evaluate retirement assets, how to access them strategically, and how to structure your finances to qualify without disrupting long-term retirement growth.

Book 3 — High-Net-Worth Asset-Based Mortgage Strategies

This book is designed for borrowers with significant assets who want to optimize leverage, preserve liquidity, and structure large or complex transactions. You will learn how wealthy borrowers qualify without traditional income and how to position assets for maximum efficiency and control.

Book 4 — Primary Residence Asset-Based Mortgage Loans

This book shows you how to purchase or refinance your primary home using assets instead of income. You will learn how to structure down payments, reserves, and loan options to maximize flexibility while maintaining long-term financial stability.

Book 5 — Investment Property Asset-Based Mortgage Loans

This book focuses on building a real estate portfolio using asset-based lending. You will learn how to qualify for multiple properties, integrate rental income, manage reserves, and scale your investments without being limited by income.

Book 6 — Securities-Based Mortgage Lending Strategies

This book explores how to use stocks, bonds, and brokerage accounts to secure financing. You will learn how to leverage investment portfolios without liquidating them, preserving growth while accessing capital for real estate opportunities.

Book 7 — Foreign National Asset-Based Mortgage Loans

This book explains how international buyers can qualify for U.S. real estate using global assets. You will learn how lenders evaluate foreign income and assets, and how to structure deals across borders with confidence.

Book 8 — Jumbo Asset-Based Mortgage Loans

This book focuses on financing high-value and luxury properties. You will learn how to structure large loan amounts, meet stricter guidelines, and position assets to qualify for jumbo financing without traditional income.

Book 9 — Asset-Based Mortgage Refinancing & Equity Access

This book teaches you how to unlock equity from existing properties using asset-based strategies. You will learn how to refinance without income, access liquidity, and use your equity to fund new investments or opportunities.

Book 10 — Advanced Asset-Based Mortgage Structuring

This book brings everything together. You will learn how to engineer approvals, layer assets, sequence transactions, and create sophisticated financing strategies that maximize flexibility, control, and long-term growth.

This series is designed to move you step-by-step from understanding to execution to mastery. By the end, you will not just know how to qualify for loans—you will understand how to control capital, structure wealth, and build a financial system that works for you long-term.

Educational & Financial Disclaimer

The *Asset-Based Mortgage Mastery Series* is intended for educational and informational purposes only. The content provided throughout this series is designed to help readers better understand asset-based mortgage lending, real estate financing strategies, and financial structuring concepts. It is not intended to be, and should not be interpreted as, financial, legal, tax, investment, or mortgage advice.

Joseph G. Correa and Live Stronger Faster are not acting as your personal financial advisor, attorney, accountant, or licensed mortgage professional in any jurisdiction through this publication. All information is presented in a general format and may not apply to your specific financial situation, goals, or circumstances. Readers are strongly encouraged to consult with qualified professionals—including licensed mortgage brokers, financial advisors, tax professionals, and attorneys—before making any financial or real estate decisions.

Mortgage lending guidelines, underwriting standards, and loan program availability vary by lender, location, and over time. Asset-based mortgage programs, including asset depletion loans and non-qualified mortgage (Non-QM) products, are subject to change without notice. The examples, strategies, and scenarios presented in this series are for illustration purposes only and do not guarantee approval, specific loan terms, or financial outcomes. Individual results will vary based on credit profile, asset structure, property type, market conditions, and lender requirements.

Real estate investing and the use of leverage involve risk. Property values can fluctuate, interest rates can change, and market conditions may impact both income and asset performance. While asset-based lending provides flexibility, it also requires careful planning, risk management, and financial discipline. Readers are responsible for evaluating their own risk tolerance and making decisions that align with their long-term financial goals.

Any references to potential income, returns, cash flow, or financial growth are not guarantees or promises of performance. These outcomes depend on multiple factors beyond the control of the author and publisher, including economic conditions, market trends, borrower decisions, and lender policies.

The author and publisher make no representations or warranties regarding the accuracy, completeness, or reliability of the information contained in this series. While every effort has been made to provide accurate and up-to-date information, errors or omissions may occur. The author and publisher disclaim any liability for losses, damages, or consequences resulting from the use or misuse of the information provided.

By reading this series, you acknowledge that you are solely responsible for your financial decisions and actions. The purpose of this content is to provide knowledge, perspective, and strategic insight—not to replace professional advice or guarantee specific outcomes.

Use this information as a guide, not a substitute for professional consultation, and always make decisions based on your individual financial situation, goals, and risk tolerance.

Risk Disclosure

The *Asset-Based Mortgage Mastery Series* discusses financial strategies involving real estate, lending, leverage, and asset-based qualification methods. These strategies involve inherent risks, and it is important that all readers fully understand and accept these risks before applying any concepts presented in this series.

Real estate markets are subject to fluctuation. Property values may rise or fall due to economic conditions, interest rate changes, local market dynamics, or unforeseen events. There is no guarantee that any property will appreciate in value or generate consistent income. Investments in real estate may result in financial loss.

The use of leverage, including mortgage financing and asset-based lending, increases both potential returns and potential risks. Borrowing against assets or property can amplify losses if market conditions change or if income from investments does not perform as expected. Failure to meet loan obligations may result in foreclosure, loss of property, or damage to credit.

Asset-based mortgage lending relies on the valuation and accessibility of financial assets. Investment accounts, retirement funds, and other assets may fluctuate in value due to market volatility. A decline in asset value may impact a borrower's financial position, liquidity, and ability to refinance or secure additional financing.

Interest rates may change over time, particularly with adjustable-rate or interest-only loan structures. Rising interest rates can increase monthly payments, reduce cash flow, and affect long-term affordability. Borrowers must be prepared for potential payment increases and plan accordingly.

Liquidity risk is another important consideration. While asset-based lending allows borrowers to qualify using assets, those assets may be tied up in investments or subject to penalties or restrictions. In times of financial stress, accessing funds may not be as immediate or favorable as expected.

Rental income and investment returns are not guaranteed. Vacancy, tenant issues, maintenance costs, property management expenses, and market conditions can all impact cash flow. Relying on projected income without accounting for these variables can create financial strain.

Refinancing and equity access strategies depend on market conditions, property values, and lender guidelines. There is no assurance that refinancing will be available in the future or that favorable terms will be offered. Changes in lending standards or economic conditions may limit access to capital.

Private lending, capital recycling, and advanced financial strategies discussed in this series involve additional layers of risk, including borrower default, insufficient collateral, and market uncertainty. These strategies require careful due diligence and risk management.

Tax laws and regulations may change over time, affecting the benefits of certain strategies such as depreciation, capital gains deferral, or asset structuring. Readers should consult with qualified tax professionals to understand how these changes may impact their financial plans.

All financial decisions involve risk, and past performance or examples presented in this series do not guarantee future results. The scenarios and illustrations provided are for educational purposes only and may not reflect actual outcomes. Individual results will vary based on personal circumstances, market conditions, and execution.

By using the information in this series, you acknowledge that you understand the risks involved and accept full responsibility for your financial decisions. The author and publisher are not liable for any losses, damages, or outcomes resulting from the application of the concepts discussed.

It is essential to approach asset-based lending and real estate investing with careful planning, professional guidance, and a clear understanding of your financial goals and risk tolerance.

www.ingramcontent.com/pod-product-compliance
Ingram Content Group UK Ltd.
Pitfield, Milton Keynes, MK11 3LW, UK
UKHW020159290926
15471UKWH00005B/959

9 798349 647765